Ajna Chakra

With kind regards, ॐ and prem

Ajna Chakra

Rishi Nityabodhananda

Yoga Publications Trust, Munger, Bihar, India

© Bihar School of Yoga 2009

Published by Yoga Publications Trust
   First edition 2009
   Reprinted 2010

ISBN: 978-81-86336-80-9

Publisher and distributor: Yoga Publications Trust, Ganga Darshan, Munger, Bihar, India.

Website: www.biharyoga.net
         www.rikhiapeeth.net

Printed at Thomson Press (India) Limited, New Delhi, 110001

Dedication

*In humility we offer this dedication to
Swami Sivananda Saraswati, who initiated
Swami Satyananda Saraswati into the secrets of yoga.*

Contents

Prologue

Karmas are what we have done, do and will do, and life is an endless series of karmas. We move through life acting out our karmas in the hope that life will improve. Life is never perfect and our hopes are for the future. We collect ideas to relieve our plight and embark on a path in the hope that we can either solve our problems or escape into a new domain free from the trammels of present day life. Just look at what we are doing, endlessly making more and more plans for the future to relieve our plight. Even when we have the best available of everything, still we make plans to escape from the agony of life. The agony is within and there is a root cause. The great thirteenth century Sufi poet, Rumi, calls it the lament: the lament of the reed flute plucked from the riverbed of reeds; it laments with the agony of being separated from its source, and the player of this reed flute also laments with his separation from his source.

And what is this source from which we come? Well it seems we don't know, or rather we have forgotten. According to our great traditions and teachings, we were once part of that source and it was a perfect seamless consciousness. According to Sufi traditions it is pure love. The love that is so pure that there are no barriers or distinctions between the lover and the beloved. It is all one; and just as the drop in the ocean is a part of the ocean and at the same time *is* the whole ocean, in the same way our origins are that drop, a part of the whole, and this is the ecstatic state of being. It is pure, it is boundless, it is unchanging and it is beyond description, yet its expression is an inspiration to ecstasy, a transport to transcendental bliss.

We know that the path is from the particular to the general, from worldly actions to inner truth, but where is this path? Is it just in the mantra and the meditation? Is it just in the karma yoga and the kirtan? After these things don't we remain with the same understandings and identifications as before? We read and we know everything, yet we have learnt that hope in external efforts is bound to end with disappointment. The successful man flying first class to Los Angeles is driven by the will to escape his longing to reunite and the subsistence farmer is driven by the same longing. We suppress our original lament. The lament is the sorrowful tune doled out in our hearts, for we have separated from our source just like the reed flute that plays its mournful tune.

Every church, synagogue, mosque, gurudwara and temple has but one altar, an altar to that one perfection, and everyone born into this world of hope takes a position or stand either acknowledging or denying its validity. Yet who has come close to it through an intellectual analysis? This draws us into a debate on faith and conviction. Faith surely holds the upper hand, the hand of experienced knowledge, knowledge gained not by intellectual conclusion but by a truth, a vision or an experience. Then we, the knower of that experience, know what is true. When a truth is so obviously definite, then faith is born and a conviction is also. Seeing the truth, or seeing the dawning of an idea which is so obviously and definitely true because it has been seen in the form of spiritual experience, is seeing through the eye of intuition, ajna chakra.

Introduction

I remember an old man from Austria who lost his father during early childhood. He attended the funeral ceremony which was a most solemn occasion, and he was so pained by the sadness of the occasion that he never visited his father's grave again. The old man had fought in the Austrian army in the First World War and stayed in his mother country until Hitler's army forced him out in 1939, when he went to England. He fought with the British army and at the end of the Second World War migrated to Australia where he finally settled down to become firmly established in that country. In 1965, sixty years after the death of his father, he made the pilgrimage back to his motherland. The pangs of his conscience were strongly telling him to visit his father's grave so that he could pay his respects to the memory of his dead father.

After some enquiries with relatives he found the cemetery, but alas, the records were incomplete and no trace of the whereabouts of his father's grave could be found in the files. His country had been ravaged by two world wars and little indeed was left from the pre-First World War era. So he set out with strong determination to systematically examine each gravestone of the huge cemetery. He started his quest in the morning and by late afternoon, in spite of his persistent efforts, he had no success. Dejected, fatigued and exhausted he sat down, and his body fell so that it was supported by his arms with his hands covering his face.

In a flash he was not an old man any more, but a young boy walking behind his father's coffin. He could see his brothers, the inscription on the coffin, the coffin bearers and all the other mourners which made up the procession. This young boy followed in the procession until it came to a hole in the ground. Then, as if coming out of a dream, he returned to waking consciousness and there he was, looking down at the gravestone which bore the inscription of his father. We can understand that this experience had exploded from the unconscious mind, but the eye which had witnessed the experience and coordinated all the movements in the physical body was his third eye or ajna chakra.

I take up this task of rewriting *Ajna Chakra* (first published in 1973) as an offering to my guru, Swami Satyananda Saraswati. Originally, around 1972, he told me to write an article and armed with some one-sided paper, a pencil and some books on kundalini yoga I just wrote down whatever I could and gave him the result. At the time he said, "I asked you to write an article and you have written a book!" At a first reading of my old work I am quite astounded at the quality of my effort then and I can only attribute this to the high level of enthusiasm I carried in my early years as a swami, the result of living with the greatest man I have ever met.

Ajna chakra is most significant amongst the whole gamut of chakras and nadis for those taking to the path of kundalini yoga. Kundalini shakti rises and energizes those parts of the personality we develop, and it is through this intuitive third eye that we can perceive the wisdom of renouncing fame, name, wealth and other worldly and passionate pursuits. Knowledge of the external world is gained through the senses; however, it is through our sixth sense, namely ajna chakra, that other knowledge is gained. There are so many things we know to be true, yet there is no evidence for it, we just know it.

We take to the path of yoga without much knowledge and in search of this knowledge we come across many traditions of spirituality, which are in essence yoga. Yoga may mean union: a unification of the individual with the superconsciousness. Some traditions are self-reliant and do not seek help from a saviour. These paths, such as Buddhism and Jainism, are paths of rigorous inner cleansing, processes of replacement of all selfish drives, ambitions and desires for selfless ones. Only by getting out of our limited selves can we expand through caring for others. It is not desire that binds us, but desire for our own limited self that leads to the things that bind us to worldly life. The process of expansion leads to enlightenment, free from any limitation.

Any discussion on ajna chakra lies within the realm of tantra, and kundalini yoga is a tantra. Tantra is dependent upon the female aspect of consciousness; she is the divine mother and it is to her that we turn to propitiate our link with divinity and to pray for progress in any tantric pursuit. We pray that we may make progress in our endeavours to awaken the shakti within and walk towards the ultimate goal.

Kundalini shakti, the primal dormant potential energy which can be awakened, resides in mooladhara chakra, the base of the subtle system of chakras. Shiva, consciousness, resides in sahasrara chakra. In the tantric macrocosmic model every part of Shiva is imbued with Shakti and every part of Shakti is imbued with Shiva. The definable phenomenal universe is Shakti and she has many energy states. Her higher energies are most subtle and her lower energy states are physical. Our state of devolution has rested in such a low state that we identify with the gross material and physical matter and have separated from the ethereal and divine. Now we see the divine as something far off to reach for and we struggle to understand it. The physical reality comes and goes, takes birth and dies, yet we look at it as if it is *the* reality.

Kundalini shakti sleeps in the form of a coiled serpent wound around the Shiva lingam three and a half times. We have managed to differentiate matter from consciousness, we have taken the spirit out of physical life and so the spirit has become dormant and an awakened shakti becomes our potential. Our consciousness has become unconscious; it is sleeping and this is our predicament.

3

With awakening of kundalini comes the dawn of our hidden powers, abilities and inner knowledge, and without some training we become lost in a sea of doubts and confusions. Our own unconscious haunts us with new images and drives; guilt, fear and violence have forced us to suppress so much and with the awakening of kundalini shakti these experiences are revived. How do we face our own internal horrors? Such awakenings are accompanied by guilt, fear and anger, and this is hard to manage in a timid and polite society.

It is for this reason that many teachers in the kundalini tradition lead their students to first take up the practices for awakening ajna chakra, the third eye, the eye of intuition. Then we can see through the confusion to the way ahead.

1

Science is Catching Up

Ancient knowledge of the laws of the universe, movement and position of stars and planets, of the macrocosmic process of creation and its correlation with the early science of creation, has been clouded by doubt. Religions and philosophers have had much to say on these subjects and their explanations have been varied, leaving the common enquirer at a loss. Meditation throws light on the problem and we can come to an understanding that apparent anomalies are nothing but stages in understanding or in development of the truth.

The nature of ultimate reality may be described as the original source from which everything, including ourselves, is created. This reality is both indescribable and the essence of everything that is manifest and knowable. Logic demands a manifest creative energy, taking its forms of creation from an unmanifest cosmic energy. Yet many over the ages have reported an unmanifest ultimate experience of just consciousness alone being the only reality. This is known as a non-dual experience in the Adwaita school of philosophy. Non-dualism emphasizes the unreality of anything but absolute consciousness, whereas monism can and does accept the existence of this manifest dimension as well as holding that there is only one absolute unmanifest dimension of consciousness out of which the universe and life has sprung. Monism has led to problems, where those fiercely holding on to their belief look at others of varying faiths and begin to fight for the validity of their faith and the falsity of others. Non-dualism cannot lead to faith in a false God or false consciousness because there is only one consciousness, and faith in anything must be in that only reality simply because it cannot be anything else.

For the ordinary person this is all intellectual; if confronted with the proposal that life and this universe are an effect without a cause, then he throws his hands up in despair. Only materialists have no problem in accepting the creation of a universe without a cause. So we have a minefield of introspection and speculation without any real evidence, barring individual experiences.

Rumi summed up this apparent anomaly with his poem, saying that the evidence is within us – it is that void within aching to reunite with our real selves. The mournful lament of the reed flute after it has been plucked from its source, the reed bed, is a symbol of the soul's sorrow at being parted from the beloved Divine.

Just as Adi Shankaracharya said that there is only one reality and different ways of describing it, in the same way Rumi also understood the apparent anomalies poetically:

The Elephant in the Dark, On the Reconciliation of Contrarieties

Not far from Ghur once stood a city tall
Whose denizens were sightless one and all.
A certain Sultan once, when passing nigh,
Had pitched his camp upon the plain hard by,
Wherein, to prove his splendour, rank, and state,
Was kept an elephant most huge and great.
Then in the townsmen's minds arose desire
To know the nature of this creature dire.
Blind delegates by blind electorate
Were therefore chosen to investigate
The beast, and each, by feeling trunk or limb,

Strove to acquire an image clear of him.
Thus each conceived a visionary whole,
And to the phantom clung with heart and soul.
When to the city they were come again,
The eager townsmen flocked to them amain.
Each one of them – wrong and misguided all –
Was eager his impressions to recall.
Asked to describe the creature's size and shape,
They spoke, while round about them, all agape,
Stamping impatiently, their comrades swarm
To hear about the monster's shape and form.
Now, for his knowledge each inquiring wight
Must trust to touch, being devoid of sight,
So he who'd only felt the creature's ear,
On being asked: 'How doth its heart appear?'
'Mighty and terrible,' at once replied,
'Like to a carpet, hard and flat and wide!'
Then he who on its trunk had laid his hand
Broke in: 'Nay, nay! I better understand!
'Tis like a water-pipe, I tell you true,
Hollow, yet deadly and destructive too.'
While he who'd had but leisure to explore
The sturdy limbs which the great beast upbore,
Exclaimed: 'No, no! To all men be it known
'Tis like a column tapered to a cone!'
Each had but known one part, and no man all;
Hence into deadly error each did fall.
No way to know the Al man's heart can find:
Can knowledge e'er accompany the blind?

Science and creation

In the face of confusion in truths couched in poetic forms
and with the evolution of logical and rational minds, scientific
knowledge has now become respected because it has either
been proved or is presented as a theory or hypothesis.
Einstein's relativity is a theory not a law, until now unproved,
yet it is commonly accepted as fact. This theory is the product

of intuition. Albert Einstein had given priority to his curiosity and imagination, and out of that came his famous theories, later validated by rational processes of mathematical logic. The first clues to a scientific understanding of creation came with the work of Roger Penrose, mathematician, University of Oxford, and Stephen Hawking, who researched black holes and pulsars. They found that matter was disappearing into nothing and inadvertently stumbled into the back door of creation. They proposed that if matter can disappear into nothing, then by the reverse process, creation, matter can appear out of nothing.

Penrose was speaking on 'Compass', a religious and spiritual production shown on ABC television in Australia. On this program, titled 'Testing God', Penrose said that there are conditions in the universe where Einstein's theories no longer hold true. In black holes and in other mysterious phenomena where the threshold limits of time and space are reached, we come to a state where time and space are extinguished, and physicists are now coming to the conclusion that it is from this point of nothing that creation emerged. Science is proposing and is in the throes of proving that creation emerged from a 'nothing' and it describes 'nothing' as pure cosmic energy independent of any creator. Scientists say that creation occurred out of a collision of the waveforms of this energy, and the first definable element created is described as a big bubble of nothing (in yoga called *akasha tattwa* or space). Current findings by scientists correlate with ancient samkhya and tantric philosophies of creation of the elements or *tattwas*.

How did Einstein come to his famous theory? Through a flash of information coming to his mind that he intuitively knew was correct. Subsequently he validated this intuitive knowledge with mathematics, a labour which took him ten years before he could present his theory to fellow scientists. How did Mahatma Gandhi know how to oppose British rule in India? Through ideas coming to his mind that he intuitively knew were the way, and history has validated the correctness of his intuitive knowledge.

8

When an idea flashes into the mind and we know it is right, it comes as intuition. When the idea is to do with the nature of the superconscious, it is called intuitive wisdom or revelation, and is the result of an intense search into the nature of God. The deep inner certainty it conveys is absolute. It comes not as a 'conclusion' to some process of thinking or reasoning, but fully developed, like the goddess Athena from the brow of Zeus. Being completely absorbed in a search for meaning, a quest for knowledge, or a sustained continuous effort to complete a task, opens the channels for intuitional knowledge to flow. When the energy level is raised through total absorption, the rational and logical mind tires of understanding and its influence recedes.

As the commentator from 'Testing God' said, "Now scientists have been looking to the heavens with the pointed stick of empirical knowledge, and God, or transcendental consciousness if you prefer, is under attack and as a result of their sustained efforts they are coming up with some remarkable findings." Not surprisingly, they have found that God does not exist within the realms of empirical knowledge and creation is the product of cosmic wave collisions. They have also come to the conclusion that this universe would not be here but for us who witness it.

Ancient seers using the eye of intuition have seen the answer, that the macrocosmic picture is twofold: one consciousness, which is all pervasive, all knowing and inactive, and one cosmic energy, which is all pervasive, all-powerful and active; or one consciousness as the only reality, and the universe and manifestations as the product of an illusory force. Neither view is arguing with the other and saying, "Mine is the way." No, this is what they saw and what they experienced and their reports have come to us, and now physicists are busy validating these intuited experiences.

Awakening of ajna chakra is opening the channel to experience the answers to those questions haunting every seeker. When the query is in the realm of the superconscious or spiritual matters, the experience of this knowledge is not only enlightening, it is memorable, it is ecstatic, blissful, and rewards the seeker with elements of wisdom.

The wisdom of the ancient sages has been passed to us through written records. These records are testaments to their spiritual experience related to us through dramatization, a conversation between student and teacher, or as an epic drama where experienced truths are related through the minds of characters within these dramas and sometimes as a straightforward, powerful description in poetic rhyme. These eloquent masterpieces, often voluminous, give evidence that ancient sages had a gift of language and a wealth of spiritual experience far in advance of any modern day sage.

Truth is in the domain of a higher mind beyond the scope of intellect, which only gives order and classification to the experienced truths. The place of the mind in the scheme of creation was clearly understood and by definition was a collection of knowledge gained by the senses and memorized. This lower mind and ordinary intellect was clearly understood to have nothing to do with experienced truth channelled through an awakened ajna chakra. Rather the norm was the opposite of today's emphasis on the intellect in the search for truth. Ancient literature is clear that the barriers to truth are created in the ordinary mind. Overcoming barriers was the path and the goal was not understanding but experience of the truth.

Big bang theory

What Penrose first calculated by reversing the equations of black hole frequency were the 'big bang' equations of the beginning of creation. Stephen Hawking subsequently verified these equations, and then in 1965 the sound of the roar of the big bang was heard. Immediately the question arose – what was God's role in all this? Physicists had shown and observed that just as matter can collapse in on itself and disappear into nothing, so also can matter spring out of nothing.

But scientists were immediately pressed by another problem: why had the big bang happened at all?

Creation has always been a matter for speculation. The Indian philosophies of Tantra and Samkhya are quite definite about creation. These philosophies state that there are two apparent realities: the manifest reality, which is subject to time and space, and the unmanifest reality, which is not. Time and space have been created out of the unmanifest, known as the transcendental or cosmic reality. Cosmic reality is indescribable and is composed of pure cosmic energy and cosmic consciousness in harmony and balance. Cosmic energy has three potentials: dynamism, balance and stagnation. These are known as the *gunas*.

Physicists have recently calculated the existence of a multitude of universes, calling them parallel universes. Universes are created by the collision of cosmic energy vibrations, and scientists are now involved in creating universes in laboratories. Two or more waveforms collide, creating an explosion of energy and a universe is created, and that universe will operate under its own unique laws. The unanswered question is how our universe with its laws of time and motion and gravity was formed out of all the billions of possibilities as if is to support life as we know it.

Physicists have calculated the series of events culminating in the creation of our universe and they agree that the universe was started by a big bang. They also theorize that before the big bang there was nothing except pure cosmic energy. There was no 'before the big bang' as neither time nor space existed. We can glimpse into the instant of big bang events in black holes and other astronomical phenomena, but scientists have not been able to calculate the exact nature of the big bang event. They have, however, determined that it was an instantaneous event and that four picoseconds (four millionths of a millionth of a second or 4×10^{-12} seconds) later the first quality of nature evolved. It was space, *akasha tattwa*.

The findings of these scientists stimulates acknowledgement of the yogic knowledge we have studied from our ancient masters. Scientists have shaken the beliefs of

11

Christian teachings, particularly in the last fifty years, yet the teachings of yoga, both ancient and modern, have not been affected.

God's role as creator has been under question ever since science has wondered about the source of the universe, and God's firm position as the foundation and source of all things has been eroding ever since. Since the beginning of thought and the quest for understanding, natural events have been attributed to God. Thunder was God's anger until we understood the nature of static electricity; pestilence was God's punishment until we understood the cause of disease. Ultimately the last remaining gap in knowledge was creation. The breakthroughs made by scientists and physicists began to make it seem that scientific enquiry, not the word of God, gave a true explanation of the creation of the universe.

In the 1960s and 70s astronomy made great advances in discovering pulsars and black holes. When pulsars were discovered, the signal was nothing like anything that had been heard before and deeper investigation provided the first clue as to where our universe had come from. Pulsars were stars with more mass than the sun, but smaller in size than the moon. Every second or so they gave a precise light pulse. What was amazing was their fantastic density: one teaspoon of matter on one of these stars was calculated to be one billion tons in weight and the gravity force involved opened up a whole new world of physics.

It seemed the universe was capable of things even Einstein had not suspected. Roger Penrose was convinced that pulsars were only the beginning, that there were things in the universe that the known laws of physics could not explain. He found singularities of infinite density known today as black holes. Black holes have enough gravity to draw in light, space and time.

In a black hole Einstein's equations run out and one reaches a singularity, the end of physics. Physicists have shown that on the way back to the beginning of time there is this singular state, and that is the Big Bang singularity.

Penrose and Hawkins' work was a revolution; they had proved that theory could explain even the beginning of the universe. So science had calculated the beginning of time and space and creation; the next task was to find the physical proof.

Scientists at Bell Laboratories, USA, were the first to hear the frequency, a lost whisper in the roar of the universe, a whisper of the moment of creation. They found that their microwave antennae had a persistent hiss. At first they thought it was pigeons living in the antennae; however, when they saw the frequency of the sound, they realized that this hiss was exactly the frequency predicted for the big bang.

Finding the microwave cosmic background, or the heat or hiss left over, certainly made astronomers much more confident that they understood the big bang and a fifteen billion year swathe of universal history. For some, this sound of the background radiation was the sound of God's absence. Science had produced a vision of a creation without a creator – scientifically there is no need to have a creator to start the creation off.

As the commentator in 'Testing God' says, "In this modern age, physics has become the satanic tempter, promising to rid us of God and answer all our questions, asking us – why prefer superstition over knowledge? Why blind faith over enquiry?"

Why but to awe, why but to keep you low and ignorant, his worshippers. Your eyes see so clear and yet are dim, perfectly be opened and cleared and you shall be as gods.

(Satan's tempting verse from John Milton's
Paradise Lost, Book IX)

But has the very certainty of science robbed us of what we most desire, a purpose for our lives and a reason for the universe?

It was believed that just 6,000 years ago God created the universe and put us on this planet Earth in the middle of it and everything rotated around us. Physics leaves us on the fringes of creation. We are not at the centre of our solar system and our galaxy is not at the centre of the universe. If the universe exists on the basis of the laws of nature and we are here riding along in the expansion of the universe for a few billion years until the sun burns out, there does not seem to be any special meaning to that.

But do we really have to accept this godless universe? Or is science's claim to victory over God premature?

Originally the big bang was considered simply an event without a cause. One could say nothing at all about what had set the event off in the first place. In order to discount God entirely scientists needed to investigate what the universe was like when it began. As the universe was very hot and opaque for the first 300,000 years it was not possible to see with a large telescope back to the instant of creation. To do that, scientists had to create the conditions at the time of the big bang.

Scientists resorted to the use of sub-atomic particle accelerators in the laboratory. Both matter and anti-matter were equally present at the time of the big bang, and there is such an accelerator at Fermilab in America where super cooled magnets are used to accelerate matter and anti-matter to the speed of light. Particles are collided in this vast particle-detecting machine. When collisions occur in the detector, it is not fragments of particles that are produced, it is pure energy.

The machine at Fermilab produces energies that were present four picoseconds after the big bang, where the temperature was millions of degrees. The numbers are beyond everyday experience. At such extreme temperatures, in line with the strange laws of quantum mechanics, the energy takes on the form of the primordial particle of the big bang. In effect the scientists are forcing into existence the very first elements of time, space and object which existed in our universe. If the scientists can create conditions like the big bang in which matter appeared out of nothing, God the creator is not needed for the explanation of the random nature of quantum physics. The particle accelerator experiment effectively replaces the role of God as the creator and the initiator of the big bang.

Quantum physics

Science realized that the void from which creation sprang is itself governed by the same principles as quantum physics. The picture of nothing is very different in the twenty-first century from the picture of nothing before the advent of quantum physics. One of the basic principles of quantum physics is the principal of uncertainty. Heisenberg's uncertainty principle says that it is impossible to measure both the position and the momentum or speed of a particle at a given moment because the 'particle' is both a wave and a particle. Because of the uncertainty principle, energy can be violated for a brief instant of time: it is possible for a particle and anti-particle to manifest out of the nothing, exist for a brief instant, violating the law of conservation of energy, then annihilating, return back into the nothing.

Scientists explain this by saying that if you could see nature on a microscopic scale, you would not see a quiescent space but quantum foam, a frothing of particles and anti-particles popping up and then annihilating again. So nothing really exists as a manifest element; creation is a series of momentary manifestations separated by a series of absences, and it is only a short and logical step to the Adwaita philosophy of Sri Adi Shankaracharya that nothing really exists and we believe in a non-existent material reality.

Physicists working at laboratories like Fermilab conclude that before the big bang there was nothing, no space, no time and no universe. Then because of quantum uncertainty, an expanding bubble of vacuum grew to enormous size, and that is the entire universe that we see. The expanding bubble of nothing is the creation of space out of nothing but cosmic energy *(shakti)*.

What particle accelerators did demonstrate is that the big bang did not need a supernatural cause. The void from which our universe sprang is in fact made of energy, positive and negative, in perfect balance, and why the big bang would have violated this balance is because nature at the quantum level can and does suffer the uncertainty of random events. More startling is that the scientists said that nothing could precede that moment. So the big bang, the moment of creation, was one random event in a timeless nothing.

Stephen Hawking says, "What lies north of the North Pole?" There is nothing, not because there is some mysterious land of nothing there, but because there is no such place as north of the North Pole, and in the same way there is no such time as before the big bang.

The big bang was the emergence of time itself. Scientists are now saying that we have the picture in the back of our mind of time smoothly flowing, but if the big bang was really the emergence of the universe, it is also the very beginning of time itself. We could also ask ourselves – where were we before we were born? Well, the body bit we can understand in a physical sense, but what about us, the indweller of the body?

Both scientists and yogis hold that the origins of the universe are explainable and observable. In the case of yogis such observations are not only possible but capable of being experienced by everyone. Resorting to the supernatural to explain a gap in knowledge is invalid and indefensible. As strange as quantum physics seems, scientists have been able to check everything with practical observations and nothing was needed to set the universe going, no ignition switch for God to press.

Human consciousness

Quantum physics replaces the God who rested on the seventh day, but science asks how a random universe could deliver everything with just the right conditions to produce human consciousness.

Intricate and amazing mathematical laws govern the universe and we do not know why the laws are as they are.

Were they there by chance or by design? So the problem of God as the creator has now been replaced with a deeper problem: namely, why do we exist and ponder on the nature of consciousness and why it is so?

The standard model of particle physics has been used for almost forty years for calculations in particle accelerators. This describes how quarks and leptons – a class of particles that includes electrons, muons and neutrinos – interact through three of the four fundamental forces: namely, electromagnetism plus the strong and weak nuclear forces.

However, the model contains seventeen parameters that must be inserted 'by hand', and physicists believe that it is only an approximation to a more fundamental theory. Moreover, the fourth fundamental force, gravity, has not yet been incorporated into the model. Models are now being proposed to replace the standard model with nineteen parameters, in continued efforts to understand the basic calculations on which the universe is governed.

For many scientists, what these parameters were was all that mattered. What they *might have been* is irrelevant. This is really metaphysics because the whole area is a little bit dubious. But a few realized that these are the questions physics had to answer.

Frank Tippler, a professor in mathematical physics, has written several scientifically controversial books on the existence of consciousness and spirit. He said that an answer had to be found and physics had to discover how the fundamentals of the universe were so finely tuned.

When such things as the proton mass are varied by a factor of two, the universe is not as we know it. The structure of long burning stars, such as the sun, cannot exist if the basics are changed very much. So the question arises – why do the constants have the values they do? This deceptively simple question rocked physics. It meant that science had to explain why the universe was the way it was.

2

Science and Religion

All people, physicists included, ponder upon the miracle of life and the wonder of the universe with conditions just right to support human and all other life forms. Physicists have been looking at why the laws are as they are and whether there is a possibility of other laws and of other universes. They have found rather a long list of special things.

For example, if gravity was just a little bit stronger, or electromagnetism a little bit weaker, or the mass of the electron just a tiny bit more, or the mass of the proton a little bit less, the universe we would see would be dramatically transformed. There probably would not be complex structures, there would not be life and we would not be sitting around pondering on the significance of it all. Only in a universe in which the values are very finely tuned can intelligent life arise.

In explaining the fine-tuning of an apparently designed universe without invoking a designer, scientists realized two other possible explanations. First of all, the overriding law of physics which is not yet discovered, called the 'theory of everything', would say there is only one logically possible universe. When this is understood, this theory of everything, then it would be understood that these fundamental constants are not fundamental at all, but that they have specific values coming from the logical structure of the theory, and there is no other possible physical theory. The theory of everything would not need arbitrary constants and functions; everything would flow logically and simply from a mathematical principle.

In the last few years physicists have discovered the cosmological constant: a number at the heart of the universe that is so strange, so ridiculously tiny, that even the most hard-core theorists fear it will never be explained. And without an explanation they will never have a theory of everything.

Instead of a theory of everything, physicists then came up with a new idea to explain why this universe was created as it is. The theory put forward was that it wasn't the only universe, there were trillions of them called parallel universes. This theory says there are universes that have all sorts of values, but we have only one universe that has just the right mix of values that allows beings like ourselves to evolve. If we could step back, we could see many universes of enormous size, many bubbles of enormous size that are universes in their own right. So it would be a multiverse. There would be as many universes as there are mixes of constants, and then it is not so remarkable that there is a universe to support human life.

This is the theory that physics currently puts up as the explanation of the designer-free universe. Another explanation is that there is only one universe and God fixed these particular constants for a purpose.

John Polkinghorn was for twenty-five years professor of mathematical physics at Cambridge University before he was ordained as a minister of the church. He found theology more interesting because potentially it is asking deeper and more interesting questions than science addresses. The fundamental difference between theology and physics is that theology answers the questions, "where do the laws of quantum mechanics come from?" and "where do all the other laws come from?" He thinks that looking at the world as a creation is a much more economic and satisfactory argument than simply supposing there are lots and lots of different universes.

Theoretical physics looks to see whether it is possible not to invoke a creator to set off creation. To an extent it has succeeded; all the technology around us is the result of physics, and this demonstrates that physicists can make progress without thinking about a divine creator deciding on a creation.

So despite agreeing that this universe is special, science and religion still stand apart. Neither can produce the ultimate proof and each sees the other explanation as more irrational than their own. The whole effort of the investigation is to get an agreement on the explanation of everything.

Bertrand Russell, renowned British philosopher, is credited with the following story. A lecturer is recounting how the world came about and a woman interrupts him and says, "You might be very clever, but I know how the world was put together." The lecturer asks, "Well, how?" She answers, "The world is sitting on an elephant and the elephant is standing on a turtle," and the lecturer replies, "What is the turtle standing on?" And the woman replies, "Oh, you can't trick me, it's turtles all the way down."

The dilemma

This explains the dilemma that we are up against. Creation depends on something, or creation is an effect which has a cause and that cause is an effect of a previous cause, and finally we have to come up with a basic something, a basic cause on which everything finally rests. Either we have an infinite regression, or otherwise we have a sort of levitating super-turtle on which everything rests. However, until science has found a complete explanation it will not rest, and to have some unexplained starting point for the creation of the universe is a religious belief and not science.

Science has to have a sort of starting point; either it is a creator, or it is a set of facts that are there because they are there, and if this universe that we know came into existence, why not other universes as well?

Proposing an infinite number of universes had a startling consequence: it meant inescapably that our universe had a chance set of laws. The only reason scientists were studying them was that our universe had by chance created them. If God had not defined our universe, what those scientists are saying is that the universe is defined by our presence in it. The implications of this are profound. For this is a scientific retreat from a theory that explains everything, to a position where the starting point for creation or the levitating super-turtle is us: I am the creator of this universe. How does this sit with our ancient knowledge?

Samkhya is a philosophy based on experience. Its original author, Rishi Kapila, gave us an explanation for the creation and evolution of the elements of the universe based on cause and effect. Subsequent commentators such as Gaudapada and Vachaspati Mishra have given reason to this philosophy, which can withstand sharp intellectual analysis.

Samkhya is a dualistic philosophy, and it holds that the foundation of creation lies in two primary elements: *purusha*, the all-knowing, unchanging soul made up of all individual souls, which is powerless to act; and *prakriti*, the pure cosmic energy in an eternal state of flux or change.

Purusha and prakriti are the cause for all subsequent events. Purusha is infinite and unchanging, whilst prakriti is infinite yet constantly changing. Purusha has the capacity to see whilst prakriti has the capacity to act, and creation has been described in Samkhya as the lame purusha helping the blind prakriti. In their primal form both purusha and prakriti are unmanifest, beyond time and space, and the pre-dominance of *rajas*, or the dynamic aspect of energy, flowing in prakriti causes the process of creation. The essence of our existence is the expression of our individual purusha and the sum total of creation is the expression of the sum total of all individual purushas. The starting point of creation is the individual soul.

Science gives up the chance of explaining why everything exists by just assuming it. Physics killed the old creator by revealing how creation occurred without him, but in attempting to explain away the coincidence of the fine-tuned design the old physics killed itself too, and in doing so it opened the door to a new more subtle understanding of physics and of God.

Physicists now say that the important thing is not distance and it is not mass; it is consciousness that seems to have evolved on this planet. Science has put us back to the point that religion has always said we were, at the centre of the universe. The miracle of creation is not that the universe exists, but that we are in it to witness it.

The study of personal experiences

To come to an understanding of the universe and its laws, and creation is the pursuit and domain of physicists. Biologists, psychologists and psychiatrists also pursue the validity of consciousness through the study of the microcosmic perspective within our own being. Current biological science now ponders on the reality of ancient revelations.

According to the scriptures, Christ's followers asked for a sign of God's existence to which Christ said, "An evil and adulterous generation seeks after a sign, and no sign will be given to it except the sign of the prophet Jonah. For as Jonah was three days and three nights in the whale's belly, so shall the son of man be three days and three nights in the heart of the earth." (*Holy Bible*, Matthew 12:40)

The people wanted proof, or at least a sign showing God's existence. Just as Jonah was resurrected out of the belly of a whale after three days, Christ was resurrected after crucifixion after three days in the tomb. But just as sceptics boldly pronounce this story as a fable due to lack of proof, are they capable of disproving it?

Ajna is the telescope capable of viewing future and past events. Time itself is a creation, and a personality of the stature of Christ surely had the capacity to view future events.

Andy Clark is a cognitive scientist trying to understand the nature of intelligence. He has a different certainty; that God is a by-product of activity in the human brain and that we carry in our brain an established pattern, which answers the inexplicable wonders of the human being and life itself by attributing the answers to these questions that do not make sense as being, "It was done by God."

For most of our lives the answer to whether God exists can be deferred, but as we grow older, the question becomes more pressing. According to Andy Clark there is nothing more horrific than knowing we are going to die, for when we die, we fall into a black hole and cease to be. This takes the meaning out of life, and for science death is certainly the end and anything that argues against it can be nothing more than a comforting story.

There are people whose faith in something beyond death is based not on religious teachings but on something which they feel is an undeniable experience. Over the years there have been countless numbers of people who have been reported as clinically dead and after some minutes they have returned to life. Science prefers the term 'near-death experience' and countless 'out of body after death' experiences have been reported where people have experienced beings both seen and the presence of a being yet unseen, and further report experiences of overwhelming compassion, light and knowledge.

They witness souls hanging on to their earthly existence, continuing in their thought patterns of old. Stockbrokers still full of tension continue to play a stock market that only exists in the realm of their own minds. Drinkers, gamblers and fighters continue with their habits, not realizing that they have lost the physical body. They report higher realms of study, of literature and poetry, and the highest realms of light, beauty, clarity and love for all mankind.

Often these experiences are in hospital, and during these experiences the person is seen to have died and after three minutes or ten minutes they return and make 'miraculous' recoveries. Further, they report that the experiences of overwhelming compassion and love stay with them for the rest of their lives, changing them forever. Reported so-called near-death experiences cover the whole gamut of experience from the most base earthly to the most heavenly and divine. By far the most common experience reported is that of the bright white light, a constant reassuring secure companion; the white light of ajna.

Some researchers have concluded that these experiences are illusions and must occur either when the person is losing consciousness or regaining it, but definitely not when clinically dead. However, many researchers are of the opinion that domains of consciousness, other than those perceivable by the ordinary senses, are a possible reality and near-death experiences are not just illusions.

Peter Fenwick is one such person. He is a neuro-psychiatrist at the Institute of Psychiatry who has been studying near-death experiences for over twenty years. He thinks there are problems with the conventional explanation. He reports that EEG measurements of the brain activity during stages of losing consciousness shows that this decay of consciousness is very rapid and could not have sufficient time for such experiences, and when the EEG is flat, none of the cortical structures of the brain function and, according to our science, this precludes the possibility of such experiences. Therefore, mainstream medicine thinks the experiences must be during recovery. However, Fenwick disagrees. He says that during arousal, while the brain is receiving oxygen, there is very confused thinking and such a brain would not be able to experience the clarity of such experiences reported.

Peter Fenwick knows that it would be unscientific to ignore the fact that thousands of unconnected people from different cultures right through the ages have had the same experiences, and he concludes that it is a fact that these are the range of phenomena that you can experience, and you have to look at these experiences and see what value you are going to put on them. Fenwick concludes that these values could be of two types: either they are cultural, or they define other dimensions of reality, and science will have to accept the validity of other dimensions of reality.

It is not just near-death experiences which persuade Fenwick that so-called subjective experiences might have more reality than science recognizes. There is also what he considers to be tantalizing evidence coming from prayer studies as well. He says that he is now finding that subjective experience can directly affect the world. If one looks at a person praying for something to happen, direct mental intent at a distance, this type of prayer does have an effect.

In the Vatican City such reports of healing through prayer do not come as a surprise. In a centuries old vault are kept the records of what they call miracles, astonishing cures that have no scientific explanation and which they attribute to the power of prayer. In order to arrive at the decision that a case is indeed a miracle, one must totally exclude any possibility of human intervention or human explanation of the case. Therefore, these cases of miracles have to be studied by scientists involved in that particular specialization of medicine. The cure, beyond any shadow of a doubt, has to be permanent and scientifically inexplicable.

Anybody who has practised pranic healing techniques will know the importance of ajna in transferring and supplying healing prana to others. This may be initiated through prayer or by mantra or through direct manipulation of prana.

Fenwick is not trying to validate the role of God in the same sense as the Vatican, but he has monitored several clinical studies in America, which appear to show that hospital patients being prayed for recover more quickly than those not being prayed for, regardless of their beliefs. Fenwick points out that the evidence for hastened healing through prayer is undeniable, yet science is making no progress because the fundamental science is flawed when it comes to research into subtle out-of-body experiences.

Subjective experience
Yogis have disciplined and concentrated their minds to experience intuitive subtle states, and in these states they have experienced five dimensions of consciousness called *koshas*.

25

They have experienced, recorded and categorized all the elements of creation from the unmanifest indefinable cosmic consciousness and the unmanifest indefinable cosmic energy to gross solid matter, beyond which there is no further creation.

The experiences have been subjectively recorded and in turn, over the ages, thousands have discovered the ancient knowledge for themselves. This metaphysical data need not be ignored on the grounds that it cannot be verified by the science of today. Science cannot accept the immeasurable and indefinable, yet scientists see the clear evidence of particles emerging from nothing; they see a reality that transcends human existence, and this reality exists when the brain is clinically dead.

It is time for science to change its approach to gaining knowledge. So far, disproving hypotheses has made great gains. Newton, Galileo and many others disproved earlier hypotheses to establish their own laws, which resisted further attempts to disprove them.

However, when researching into the source of everything, the subtlest of the subtle, the unmanifest and indefinable, which is immortal consciousness beyond time and beyond space, the basic attitude must be of acceptance, and when this acceptance takes place, the scientist becomes a yogi. By accepting the validity of other dimensions of consciousness beyond objective external reality, we can witness and experience such dimensions. Then the scientist makes his body a laboratory, his mind the instrument of research and his experience the result and conclusion. The conclusion is that there is a theory of everything, the macroscopic creation is a reflection of that domain called superconsciousness in which we know everything, and all this is known through the quality of our subtle eye, otherwise known as ajna. Only then can the experience stand the test of intellectual analysis.

3

Philosophical Background

Ajna chakra is part of the psychic physiology described in kundalini tantra, amongst the teachings of tantra, an integral division of Indian philosophy. Indian philosophies in general and tantra in particular have not been authored by thinkers, but by those who have transcended the constraints of the ordinary mind and experienced higher levels of consciousness and energy.

The books on those experiences tell us that beyond the ordinary intellect there is another source of knowledge. They call it a higher state of consciousness. This consciousness transcends the ordinary conscious mind and is termed cosmic or superconsciousness.

Original texts emphasize that the ordinary state of mind or waking consciousness is pale in comparison. Since ancient times highly evolved souls have experienced the awakening of kundalini. Seekers have followed the paths laid down and have seen and experienced subtle aspects of the body, mind, chakras and universe, and then subsequently reported them to us. These reported experiences give us a clear vision of our psychic physiology and internal symbols associated with each level of consciousness.

The reports are in the form of manuscripts called tantras and in total make up the tantra shastras. Descriptions are lucid and there is a concordance amongst the vast array of tantras on any one subject by different authors. For example,

27

there are numerous descriptions of ajna chakra and the symbols seen within it. Most of the kundalini tantras agree that in ajna or bhru chakra resides a goddess named Hakini who has four arms and drinks ambrosia. Experiences of higher consciousness and kundalini descriptions have been written down in a variety of texts spanning thousands of years, yet they are basically the same with varying terminology.

Therefore, we can rely on the instructions, methods and mantras written down by those who have walked the path before us. No doubt the experiences they report are spiritual and beyond the realm of the senses. The validity of spiritual experiences cannot be measured by the logic of worldly, material or sensorial experiences because they are of different realms. Material experiences are dependent on an object perceived by the senses whereas spiritual experiences are beyond the senses. It is pointless to argue the validity of spiritual experiences from a materialistic point of view.

In space things are not what they appear to be: straight lines become curved, space is curved, and mass and time are a function of the speed in relation to the speed of light. In the same way, we have to accept the validity of spiritual experiences. Because everyone does not encounter spiritual reality does not mean that it is not there; it just means the few who have broken the bonds with worldly existence have experienced the spiritual reality, in the same way that the few who have broken away from the pull of earth's gravity know what it is like to be in space.

Mandukya Upanishad tells us that objective reality, the reality that we know in our ordinary waking state, has manifested from a higher energy state, an unmanifest reality. Just as the apple tree is the manifestation of the essence of the apple seed, this creation is a manifestation of higher reality. All these things have been seen and experienced in lucid encounters with higher reality. Higher reality is often described in poetic and often dramatized passages. These passages are ultimately written and subsequently categorized in volumes that make up the Indian philosophical systems.

Mandukya Upanishad describes the experience from the microcosm of individual consciousness, yet it describes the whole creation manifesting from the macrocosmic super-conscious state. It is here that we come to understand that the universal macrocosm is the same as the individual microcosm, and that individual consciousness is not an ultimate reality.

The ultimate consciousness, called *turiya*, is not that which is conscious of the inner (subjective) world, nor that which is conscious of the outer (objective) world, nor that which is conscious of both, nor that which is a mass of consciousness. It is unperceived, unrelated, incomprehensible, uninferable, unthinkable and indescribable. The essence of the consciousness manifesting as the self (in the three states), it is the cessation of all phenomena; it is all peace, all bliss and non-dual. This is what is known as the fourth; this is *atman* (self), and this has to be realized.

We must note at this point that the word philosophy is English for the Sanskrit word darshan. *Darshan* means that which is revealed or seen; a vision of the divine or sacred or truth. Often darshan is the vision of a manifest divine. The vision of Christ three days after his crucifixion is called darshan, and the sacred texts are considered as darshan because their content has been seen.

Adepts sitting steady for long periods using mantras and concentration techniques, transcend body and mind to access the turiya state and then darshan or revelations of that state are experienced. The revelations outlined the path and gave aspirants purpose and inspiration. In turn others have experienced these revealed truths.

Kundalini tantra is the truth about the complex psychic human physiology, about its dormant potential as well as the means to awaken kundalini shakti, the store of energy, and the levels of awakening according to the chakras. Descriptions of the chakras detail multi-petalled flowers with yantras, mantras, colours and deities, and these descriptions have made an indelible mark in the psyche of all those who have come across such information.

Sanatana dharma

In ancient times, before the idea of categorizing people into different religious groups, communities around the Indus River were organized in such a way as to guide people towards inner spiritual experience. Wealth and greatness were measured in terms of spiritual attainment and materialistic goals were understood to support materialistic needs. Spiritual life was balanced with worldly life, and life was divided into four stages. The first stage was childhood and youth dedicated to education and learning, known as *brahmacharya*.

Education was broad; it included language, mathematics and social sciences, as well as spiritual lore. Very little was written; however, the *Rig Veda*, one of the oldest records of those times, sings praises of the mighty river Indus that watered fertile flood plains, providing food for so many. Records of Indus script found on thousands of tablets remain a mystery. However, archaeological excavations have unearthed a clear picture of organized communities systematically housed according to precise planning, complete with streets and roads, drainage, bathing and common facilities. With the passing of time the Indus dried up and the communities migrated to the Ganges and other plains; however, their traditions were etched into society.

Memory was the basis of learning: thousands of books were remembered so well that when writing came into vogue some thousands of years later, the same recitations from different parts of India varied in just one or two lines over some hundreds of thousands of verses. Writing vedas and upanishads and other great texts were scribed when it was foreseen that subsequent civilizations would forget the teachings and memory would become dim.

The second stage in life was for marriage and family. This division, termed *grihastha* or householder, was society's provider. From the age of twenty-five to fifty years people pursued this window of opportunity to explore their ambitions and desires, knowing it would soon end and that all would be passed on to the next generation. However, the education gave adherents the stability to know that the highest goal, pursuit of inner experience, remained a part of their existence, and emphasis on this goal was to grow in subsequent stages.

The third stage of twenty-five years, *vanaprastha*, was training for renunciation of all worldly desires and external pursuits. Husband and wife would move to a hut in the forest and perform devotions and meditations away from emotional and material support of friends and family.

The fourth and final stage of life, termed *sannyasa*, was taken from the age of seventy-five years. This stage was a life of simplicity, austerity and contemplation combined with total renunciation of all family and friends so that all bonds could be broken.

Society was structured to turn its members away from the comforts of wealth and worldly achievement and toward spiritual perfection. This lifestyle, which encouraged evolution, was named *sanatana dharma*, meaning eternal culture. Sanatana dharma was the basic philosophy of life and now it is incorrectly described as the Hindu religion.

According to *Encyclopaedia Britannica* the British introduced the term 'Hinduism' during the 1800s in order to separate Buddhists and Sikhs from Hindus as all three faiths are based on sanatana dharma. The term Hindu originated from the Indus river and Hindus were those people whose lifestyle had originated around the Indus valley, even though the river had disappeared many thousands of years before and all that remained were the archaeological digs in the deserts of India and Pakistan, somewhat north of what is now known as Mumbai.

This sanatana culture produced a plethora of ascetic seers, as well as rishis who had families and renunciate saints. These great souls *(mahatmas)* were given the highest status; often they were advisers to kings and their influence on society was enormous. The work of saints was funded with the patronage of kings and thus the messages of these great souls are still available today.

31

Just as a flower has attractiveness and scent, in the same way saints have that quality of the divine, which is beautiful and attractive. It is to these advanced souls that the highest respect was given. Their advice was sought in all matters of state as well as in personal problems. They bequeathed mankind a large wealth of records for our guidance. Literally thousands of texts on every facet of sacred lore are available.

These records were in the form of poetic verse, illustrating the experience of the absolute through drama and question and answer. The richness of language and beauty of description composed in rhyming verse is evidence of the supreme level of mental evolution that these masters of the past had reached. This is why we hear the ring of truth in their writings; this is why we reach sublime depths of peaceful contemplation after we chant their mantras and this is why we aspire for their experience, knowing their truth to be the truth just by a whisper of acknowledgement from within us, a vibration nodding in agreement with what they have presented to us.

Thus the sanatana dharma tradition was born: teachings in the form of vedas, upanishads, epics such as the *Mahabharata* and the *Ramayana*, philosophies such as Tantra, Vedanta and Samkhya, and practical instructions in the form of kundalini yoga, hatha yoga, bhakti yoga, raja yoga, mantra yoga and laya yoga.

This system for society was based on one principle: human spirit is who we are in reality. This was the experience of sages throughout history and in identifying with the body, senses, possessions and materialistic gains, we forget who we are – the spirit.

Search for truth

Loss of memory of who we really are is illustrated beautifully in chapter four of the *Srimad Bhagavatam*. Narada relates this story to the sorrowful King Prachinabarhis, who is in search of the way to truth. "I will tell you a story," began Narada, "which illustrates in allegory what I wish to teach.

"There lived a well-known king, named Puranjana. He had an intimate friend, but none knew his name or his occupation. Puranjana roamed all over the earth, hoping to find a suitable place to live in. But he met only with disappointment. He thought to himself, I have seen many cities, but none appears good to me. I want to live in a city where all my desires may be satisfied, but none of these would be sufficient for the purpose.

"At last he came to a city in Bharatavarsha, south of the Himalayas. This magnificent city, with its nine gates, its stately palaces, its beautiful gardens and crystal lakes, appeared to have all the advantages he had been seeking. He felt that his wanderings were over, for here all his desires could be gratified.

"Then, one day soon after, Puranjana saw a beautiful young girl with her attendants, walking in a garden. Their paths met, they fell in love and within a short time they were married. They continued to live in the city of nine gates, and it was by passing through these gates that Puranjana found he could indulge his many desires, although, strange to say, he never found any real satisfaction in so doing. He loved his wife deeply and was happy only in her presence. He made her wishes his, and when she wept he wept, when she smiled he smiled. Thus slavishly responsive to her every whim and mood, he was on the way to losing the last vestige of his independence.

"For many years he stayed on in that beautiful city, gratifying his every desire but never obtaining any lasting pleasure or comfort from his way of life.

"Now it happened that while King Puranjana, immersed in pleasures, was forgetful of everything else, a mighty general attacked the city where he dwelt. This general possessed a certain magical charm by means of which he had the power to work great havoc. So it was that he demolished the beautiful city of nine gates. Puranjana himself could not escape. He found himself bereft of everything, even of that last stronghold of consciousness, his memory. He forgot well nigh all his past, his kingship and his magnificent city. One memory alone was left: the thought of his beautiful wife. This thought possessed his mind with such intensity that he did not notice his loss of memory for the rest of the world. His whole nature became obsessed by her image, and like a madman, who losing his own identity becomes the being whose image possesses him, Puranjana found himself transformed into a lovely young girl like his wife.

"The young girl he had now become forgot her previous identity to such an extent that when she met with King Malayadhvaja, she fell in love with him and married him. When in the course of time the king passed away and she was left alone, lamenting his death and her bereavement, an unknown brahmin came to her and said:

"O my beloved friend, why are you grieving? Do you not know me, your dear friend? Try to remember who and what you are. I have been your friend always, but you neglected me and forgetting me entirely went away in search of pleasure and enjoyment. You and I are friends, united in eternal bonds. Though you forgot me, I have been with you all the time. You entered into a city of nine gates and became so deeply attached to a woman that you forgot your real self. Then later you became forgetful of your past and believed yourself to be the wife of this man. You are neither the husband nor the wife. There is no sex in you. You and I are not separate. Know yourself as me. Just as one sees oneself as two when reflected in a mirror, so do you appear as you and me, but in reality we are one."

Prachinabarhis requested Narada to explain the allegory, and Narada, assenting, thus spoke on: "O King, Puranjana in the story stands for the *purusha*, the divine self. He is called Puranjana because the divine self is the manifestor of *pura*, or the body. The unknown friend that I have mentioned is *Brahman*, or God. None knows Him, for no deeds or attributes can express or reveal Him.

"The puras, or bodies, are of various kinds. Of these the human body is a suitable instrument for the enjoyment of all desires. This human body is the city with nine gates, such as eyes, ears, nose etc., through which the divine self or Puranjana goes out, as it were, to enjoy the objects of the senses. The wife is the intellect, united with whom man enjoys the world and worldly goods. In thus identifying itself with the intellect or ego, the divine self forgets its true nature and becomes immersed in ignorance and vanity. The great general is all-destructive time whose charms are disease and death; disease and death ultimately destroy this body.

"Man is divine and free and blissful. Being deluded, he superimposes the attributes of the non-self upon the self. Hunger and thirst belong to the prana, lust or desire belongs to the senses and the mind; but all these are attributed to the self in man, who is by nature free.

"Forgetful of his true divine nature, identifying himself with the false ego, man becomes attached to the world and the pleasures of the world. He then is bound by his deeds. As are his deeds, so is his birth."

This is the story of King Prachinabarhis and it is everyone's story. Spiritual aspirants are by definition dissatisfied with pleasures and worldly objectives. Thus they search for truth, a meaningful, satisfying, non-decaying truth, a truth we feel is there, yet we have lost our memory of it. Even if God comes to us in the form of experience, we will not recognize Him because our memory is dim.

Kundalini yoga

The *Srimad Bhagavatam* tells us in chapter two of the yogi who aspires to return to the memory of purusha by kundalini yoga. "A true yogi, realizing the approach of death, sits calmly in a yoga posture, and with his heart purified and mind under perfect control, becomes absorbed in the consciousness of Brahman. Thus he lives in a state of perfect tranquillity.

"Time, the great destroyer, which lords it over everything in the universe, is annihilated. The universe itself melts into nothingness. The yogi is no longer aware of his physical self.

35

The worshipful Lord Vishnu alone is in his heart. All to him is God. Such is his blissful state.

"Desiring to give up the body, he allows the vital energy to pass through the different centres of consciousness. First, the energy is concentrated in the solar plexus, called *manipura*. From there the energy rises to *anahata*, the heart. It then passes to the centre near the throat, called *vishuddhi*. From there it ascends to *ajna*, the centre between the eyebrows.

"At this point one of two things may come to pass. If the yogi has reached the state of desirelessness, he realizes the absolute Brahman and the vital energy ascends to *sahasrara*, the thousand-petalled lotus centre in the brain, called the doorway to Brahman. Then the yogi, realizing his unity with Brahman, completes the separation of himself from the senses, the sense organs, the mind and the body and passes away. He attains what is known as absolute freedom. This is called immediate liberation.

"If, on the other hand, having raised his vital energy to the centre between the eyebrows, the yogi still has some desires left in him, he does not realize the absolute unity, but passes away still associating himself with the mind and the senses. He then ascends to higher and higher lokas and ultimately reaches the brahma loka. There he becomes freed from all desires and realizes his unity with Brahman; and thus, having attained absolute freedom, there is for him no more return. This is called the gradual liberation.

"Be ye therefore, O King, a yogi, for by worshipping the lord of love one has all desires fulfilled and in the end attains freedom. Even hearing of God stimulates the higher consciousness and brings about detachment from the fleeting world. So should a man follow the path of freedom, the path of love."

Ajna chakra

Ajna is the fulcrum about which our spiritual and material lives are balanced. By identification with external values, our vision is blind to the greater truths within and this process continues until we have seen through the host of beliefs we have adopted in our hope for enjoyment and satisfaction in our materialistic lifestyle.

According to the vedantic theory of yoga and the experience of people who have perfected it, ajna chakra is the place where the greater mind manifests in the form of a desire. That desire, which is the first manifestation of the greater mind, is known as *ichcha shakti*. The greater mind next manifests in the form of willpower known as *sankalpa shakti*. Then it manifests as a creative process known as *kriya shakti*. That creative process of the supreme intelligence is later on perceived at the level of the different chakras.

Ajna chakra is a point where the higher intelligence, the unmanifest and the manifest intelligence, are both experienced. Therefore, the yogic traditions have called ajna chakra the seat of intuition, the seat of the guru or the seat of the sixth sense. The five senses belong to the manifest dimension, the manifest experience. The sixth sense, or the intuitive experience, is the transcendental manifestation of the supreme intelligence. It is here that we have to focus our creativity, willpower and desire to either be a receiver of, or a receptacle for, the manifest or unmanifest experiences.

Ajna works like a radar; what is received depends on the direction of focus. If you focus downwards, you will receive the experiences contained in vishuddhi, anahata, manipura, swadhisthana and mooladhara. The purpose of awakening ajna is to become aware of these different levels in ajna when it is focused downwards.

When you reverse the focus of ajna, then it becomes the practice of ajna dharana, which is a re-focusing of the antenna which receives information and vibrations from above. There has to be a focus for that antenna in order to channel the supreme consciousness in the form of a beam and direct it to ajna, so that the information can be received as a transcendental input into the human frame.

We have the choice either to direct our focus toward inner or transcendental knowledge, or to increase our knowledge of the aspects attributed to the qualities of the lower chakras. Once ajna is awake, we can clearly see, but without this clear sight there is no choice and we are driven by the force of our minds and our karmas. Our vision is so limited and our memory of the truth is so remote that we resort to books and other indirect sources to search for higher knowledge that we somehow know is there, but cannot see that it is there.

Today's mind is basically rational and demands proof. Knowledge based on experience is not demonstrable nor is it repeatable, and therefore science has searched the universe for the knowledge of creation. Surprisingly enough scientists have come up with correlations between what has been written in ancient texts and what is understood to be the forefront of metaphysics. The ancient knowledge was perceived through the intuitive eye of ajna, whilst the current run of science is perceived in huge laboratories.

4

The Guru Chakra

In the previous chapter the story from the epic *Srimad Bhagavatam* was told. The great sage King Puranjana was dissatisfied, yet he was united with the absolute consciousness. He sought identification with the body and its senses as a source of pleasure. He was deluded by an idea, an idea born on the urging of tamas to seek out a pleasant life. The sway of tamas was so great that in identifying with the body and its endless wishes, he obliterated the memory of being one with the nameless universal consciousness.

From the viewpoint of an ordinary seeker in the twenty-first century, on first examination this story is a contradiction in terms. It flies in the face of reason for pursuit of spiritual life. The very reason we pursue a spiritual path is to reach the ultimate state of bliss and contentment, a state where there is no dissatisfaction. King Puranjana was at one with absolute consciousness, he was one with everything; he would have realized the illusory nature of the lower self and he would have seen illusion shrouding the truth. He would have had the innate quality that comes with a fully awakened ajna chakra. He would have seen the mind, and the ramifications of such an action as identification with the body would have been plainly obvious.

Just as we would say no to an ordinary sweet from the local corner shop when we could have a box of the finest Belgian chocolate, we would expect King Puranjana to say no to lower forms of identification, yet he went ahead and ignored his identification with the ultimate, and instead identified with the body.

It is from this story that we can get an idea of why creation happened at all. This logical argument falls down only because we are missing vital information. The fact is that creation did occur, and according to science it occurred four billion years ago. It is just that together with this creation the unmanifest transformed, becoming both manifest and unmanifest. This has been spelt out in the first verse of the *Ishavasya Upanishad*. This creation manifested and its source was the unmanifest, just as rain is sourced from the ocean but the ocean does not diminish. The unmanifest remains unchanged and we have both manifest and unmanifest.

From the revelations of ancient rishis who have accessed the source of all knowledge, we know that in the ultimate unmanifest reality time stands still and there is no creation. Shiva, the absolute almighty omnipresent consciousness, is in perfect harmony with Shakti, the cosmic energy; both are unmanifest, in perfect balance and equipoise. Shakti is not a placid cosmic high energy state described by physicists as The Nothing.

Tantra – consciousness and energy

Swami Satyasangananda Saraswati, in her book *Sri Vijnana Bhairava Tantra (SVBT)*, writes: "Tantric philosophy postulates that the universe of matter and energy has evolved out of primordial nature, or Shakti, who represents pure energy. Her cosmic counterpart and co-creator is Shiva, or pure consciousness, who exists as conscious intelligence distinct from her and her derivatives. In the original state Shiva is forever immanent and eternal but inactive as opposed to Shakti, who is forever immanent and eternal but active.

"Although Shiva and Shakti separate momentarily, giving rise to the individual consciousness, in their cosmic manifestation they forever exist side by side. So there are both cosmic and individual aspects of Shiva and Shakti."

Now this begs the question: why did the momentary separation happen or why did creation and the fate of King Puranjana eventuate? Continuing with Swami Satsangi's passage on creation:

"Shiva and Shakti together give rise to the *avyakta* or unmanifest cosmos, as well as the *vyakta* or manifest creation. The first manifestations of creation are known as nada, bindu and kalaa. *Nada* literally means 'vibration'. As a part of the unmanifest creation, it exists as the cosmic vibration or *spandan*. In the vyakta or manifest creation, it exists as sound of varying frequencies. *Bindu* represents a point or nucleus, and *kalaa* is a ray or force which emanates from the nucleus, or bindu, due to the vibrations created by nada."

So here we have the seed of the answer to the whole creation question. Why do we identify with external values, knowing that truth is within? Just as water always runs downhill, our consciousness, if left to the forces of nature, moves away from ultimate wisdom towards ignorance. To move towards truth, we need a representative of the unmanifest reality pointing the way and this representative communicates with us through the guru chakra, ajna.

Out of the interplay of these qualities the limited dimension manifests, and this limited manifest dimension inherits the qualities of which it came from, namely nada, bindu, and kalaa. Atomic physics partly concurs. Heisenberg's uncertainty principle states that a subatomic particle behaves both as a particle and a wave because the energy from which subatomic particles manifested had those potentials. The energy of such particles is measured as discrete packets called quanta. Why does this manifestation always move from an undefinable subtle state to a limited dimension and why has it been happening for millions of years? This is one of the great mysteries that continue to baffle our reasonable minds because the answer is unreasonable, yet we demand an answer for such a haunting question as to why creation and us, both you and me, came into existence at all.

41

Just as my body is the manifest expression of my parents' desire, my being is the manifest expression of my desire, and creation is the manifest expression of a universal desire. The unmanifest is not at equipoise; it is energy having different qualities and at any one time one quality predominates, then at other times another of the three predominates.

Yogis following the path of tantra raised the energy within the framework of their individual awareness and uniting with universal consciousness brought enlightenment within. This was their experience and they had direct knowledge of the nature of cosmic energy. Yogis experience pure cosmic energy and have reported their experiences to us. In *SVBT* Swami Satsangi translates the original sloka (verse four) telling us of the nada, bindu and *anahata nada*, the sound that is experienced out of an invisible source, the unstruck sound.

SVBT tells us that energy is the face of consciousness. God is faceless, invisible and unmanifest, yet we can experience or reach the experience of consciousness by relating with the forms of energy, be they gross material forms *(apara shakti)*, mental or visualized form *(parapara shakti)* or supreme primal transcendent energy *(para shakti)*. *SVBT* tells us that kalaa, bindu and nada are the first evolutes of primal energy *(spandan)* in the process of creation and since nothing comes from nothing, the potential for these evolutes must be inherent in the nature of pure energy itself.

Tantra postulates that Shakti and Shiva are one. Every part of consciousness is replete with energy and the highest state of consciousness is a very high state of energy. At the moment of creation, or four picoseconds after the instant of creation, space was created and began to expand (described as an expanding bubble of vacuum). Now scientists have further calculated that this expanding bubble of universal proportion is still expanding, yet the rate of expansion is decreasing and is coming to a halt. Then it will begin to turn in on itself and shrink to an incredibly dense ball, tending toward zero dimension. This is the course of nature, indicating that the pursuit of the manifest dimension brings no ultimate reward.

Manifest dimension

Thinking humans know that worldly pursuits can only bring ongoing duties and responsibilities, and ultimately there is no joy in material gain, yet the attraction is irresistible. *Maya* is the illusory force of nature that makes us find worldly objects and attainments so attractive. Ajna is the eye that can reveal the way to a lasting satisfied bliss free from the need of objects.

Swami Niranjanananda Saraswati tells the story of Maya, the goddess of illusion, and Bhakti, the goddess of devotion, leading us to the ultimate truth. He tells us that originally Maya was dressed in unattractive rags and Bhakti was resplendent in fine clothes and jewels. One day Maya and Bhakti were at the pond and while Bhakti was busy bathing, Maya crept ashore and stole Bhakti's clothes, leaving her own rags behind for Bhakti to wear. Since then Maya's attraction is unparalleled, whilst Bhakti's beauty is concealed in rags.

So nature, the female aspect, manifests and after a time this manifestation shrinks to non-existence in the manifest dimension, yet the unmanifest dimension remains unaffected, unchanged throughout the process of creation and destruction. In the unmanifest dimension we have cosmic energy with the potential to vibrate, to behave like a point and to act like a wave, and it is a very high energy state. Just as high voltage electrical energy in clouds is naturally released as lightning, creation of the manifest dimension is a natural event.

The manifest quality of Shakti is nature, everything around us, and it is constantly changing: air, trees, rivers, earth, rocks, mountains and the absorbing blue of the sky. We are also that nature and we are also ever changing. Tantra, Samkhya and Vedanta philosophies tell us that the change in nature is due to the *gunas,* or three qualities of nature, namely, *sattwa*, *rajas* and *tamas*. Sattwa is born of the equipoise of rajas and tamas and is our highest and purest state. Just as pure unmanifest cosmic energy has its three qualities of nada, kala and bindu, manifest energy has these three qualities of the gunas.

Dominance of sattwa over the other two is our refuge from a life overwhelmed by events. Sattwa is the poetry of truth, of beauty, a love of purity, free from the trammels of worldly responsibilities and the travails of the ordinary day. Sattwa can be achieved through fasting, pilgrimages to sacred sites and through extended and continual yoga practices such as pranayama and meditation. These are well known techniques, yet the technique we use most often, but remain ignorant of, is plain hard work. Lifting rocks and stones, carrying them some distance and then digging them in to make a wall requires determination and muscles. This kind of work leads quickly to exhaustion, especially if the loads are heavy, and so we stop to rest. Then we see a bird, a leaf, an ant, or the sky and at this moment we need nothing; the blueness of the sky or the movement of the ant occupies our total attention and we become momentarily enraptured in the beauty of the moment. This is the experience of sattwic energy, a momentary equanimity or enrapture in the beauty of the moment.

Dominance of rajas manifests as our will and dynamism, as our ambition to succeed, achieve and acquire. The very core of our being, the essential consciousness, may be indefinable, all knowing, yet the energy of our being is the knowable aspect and this has the nature of the macrocosmic energy of creation from which we are manifest. Thus the dynamism of our being is a mark of our personality.

Tamas is the quality of nature that, predominating, leads to nature's own destruction. Within our own individual microcosm we have preferred solid objects to mental ideas. Prior to the creation of the body and senses we possessed, and still possess, the same faculties in the subtle dimension. In place of sight we preferred to have eyes that have the sight and then we could say, 'these are my eyes and I see', and the same goes for all the sense organs and all the organs of action. When we examine the complete process of manifestation of creation from both macrocosmic and microcosmic points of view, we come to understand that each manifestation is a process of tamas predominating.

It is little wonder that we are helplessly dragged along in the current of natural energy flow and the helpless dragging is not done by an external force. It is our own belief that pursuit of worldly actions will bring relief to the anguish of life. From birth we have been trained for worldly pursuit by our parents and peers, but this does not validate it as a spiritual path.

We took birth for a purpose: we came because we wanted to and our individual set of desires will never be exhausted until we act. According to the law of karma such unfulfilled desires can never be eliminated through superimposition of higher spiritual values and actions, and in fact pursuit of higher spiritual actions, denying the demands of our worldly ambitions and hopes, will lead to frustration on both paths, worldly and spiritual.

Role of guru

Gurus make great strides towards evolving their personality; they have disciplined minds that do not dwell on worldly directions and achievements; they have made the leap to spiritual directions and are firmly established on that path. We strive to evolve toward perfecting all our faculties and to exclude identification with our worldliness.

It is only through the continued influence of the guru for many years that we remain on our spiritual path whilst attending to our residual worldly needs. It is partly through the senses that we absorb guru's guidance and this sensory information is made up of the whole gamut of worldly influences as well. This influence comes through external means and through influence in conscious thought as well as dream, and it is these subtle communications that come to us via ajna. Information received through the five sensory channels has to compete with all worldly trends. The sacrifice of selfish and worldly gain is a part of spiritual life and the guru's influence is necessary to sustain selfless pursuit.

Guru communicates through ajna to mind, to *manas*. Guru communicates directly with mind itself and we receive this guidance as if we are thinking it ourselves, as if we are having the idea. Just as the nose is the channel through which a particular part of the mind receives smell, in the same way manas receives super sensory information from the mind itself. The part of the mind that receives information is connected to ajna and the capacity to receive super sensory information depends on the awakening of ajna or the faculties associated with ajna.

There are no psychic or personal barriers between humans when there is love between them. Such super sensory communication is an everyday occurrence with mothers and their babies and with guru and disciple. This is why there is such high praise for guru. Aspirants for spiritual life take initiation from a guru and establish a relation with that guru that is second to none. The guru's attitude toward the disciple can be remote, dismissive or autocratic; however, this behaviour is effected only after guru and disciple both have achieved such a connection that the disciple adores the guru no matter how he appears. No matter if the guru appears angry, unjust, biased, or mistaken, the disciple accepts his guru as he is. We chant *Guru Brahma, Guru Vishnu, Guru Maheshwara* (guru is the God of creation, guru is the God of preservation and guru is the God of destruction) and for the disciple if the guru appears unjust, then so be it; God is unjust also. To not accept behavioural anomalies in the guru is a separation from him and a separation from his teachings and a separation from the guru within.

The mother who finds fault in her baby distances herself from her baby at the cost of psychic communication. The husband who finds fault with his wife suffers the same distance, losing psychic communication. The same relationship capabilities are available to all humanity and it is this relationship between guru and disciple that opens the path. A disciple accepts everything in the guru's personality to keep the communication of the intuitive psychic centre.

5

Kundalini Yoga in Brief

Tantra describes the awakening of kundalini as the awakening of our dormant potential, the enormous potential within us that has not been developed. Psychologists would say that these potentials lie within the unconscious mind and *can be* developed. In our daily life we cultivate external skills in dealing with others, through the development of internal potentials, by means of intuition and being motivated through compassion: recognition of the need of others as if it were our need. This psychological approach to awakening kundalini is pursued in karma yoga and is recognized as an essential part of every sadhaka's life.

As the awakening takes place there is a parallel process occurring in the psychic dimension of the personality. The description of this psychic process and the pursuit of the awakening of dormant energy is kundalini yoga; and this is described throughout the sacred Indian texts.

Ancient seers first reported their experiences in verse form, known as *darshan*, revelations. Kundalini yoga is described in many of these darshans, including the tantras, puranas, upanishads and classic texts such as *Devi Bhagavatam*. Whilst the general principles of kundalini are common to all texts, minor points do vary since darshan is a subjective experience observed within each seer's personality.

The religiously devout, the Vedantins, Buddhists and the monotheists have all described the awakening of kundalini in their own terms. Adi Shankaracharya himself has stated that in order to realize the highest consciousness we must first awaken kundalini shakti. In *Saundarya Lahari* he poetically described this awakening:

Thou art diverting thyself in secrecy
with thy Lord in the thousand-petalled lotus.
Having pierced through the earth, situated in the mooladhara,
the water in swadhisthana, the fire abiding in the manipura,
the air in the heart (anahata), the ether above (vishuddhi),
and manas between the eyebrows (ajna),
and thus broken through the entire kula path (sushumna).

Adi Shankaracharya was an ardent and fundamental seer of Adwaita philosophy and whilst he was known for upholding that the only truth was the one fundamental consciousness, that anything else was false and illusory, he yet worshipped the mother as nature in all her infinite forms as the great consort of Shiva himself. From our point of view kundalini is in conflict with Adwaita Vedanta; that is to say that if there is only one truth and that is formless consciousness, then to worship anything else with form or name is false. Buddha held a similar vision of the truth, yet in his tradition the mother is worshipped and kundalini yoga has been practised extensively. Indeed, at a recent Goddess Exhibition in Sydney of the female divine art forms, Buddhist and Hindu representations stood side by side and were almost indistinguishable. So we, the seekers, are left with the problem of reconciliation of the truth as formless or with form.

Fortunately we are helped by way of a few quotes. Shankaracharya says, "There is only one truth and many ways of seeing it," and in the opening verses of the twelfth chapter of the *Bhagavad Gita*, Lord Krishna explains that both paths are valid and that the path of the formless is difficult. Ramakrishna Paramahamsa was a renowned worshipper of the female goddess Kali and he also gave testimony to the need of kundalini yoga.

We can conclude that kundalini is not an exclusive spiritual path and the practitioners of kundalini yoga do not exclude other practices, nor do they cling to the belief that their practice is superior to other spiritual pursuits.

Kundalini yoga states that as we evolve we do more than awaken unconscious thoughts and understanding of our situation in the world; we also awaken a power that brings abilities and capacities to the personality. A student may study medicine for many years and achieve very high qualifications, yet if he has not awakened feelings for the sufferings of those who come before him, he will be incapable of feeling any more than a technical relationship for the problems of his patients, and so he will be ineffective as a doctor; he will have no genuine driving force to become a doctor. Maybe there are more personal needs to provide for his family, needs that are the basic driving forces, which are not highly evolved and are common to all but the most primitive of our species.

Awakening of shakti

The awakening of shakti brings power to the personality in various ways according to the traits developing. This shakti has to travel on certain paths around the body. It is said there are 76,000 paths or *nadis* in the body, yet these are subtle and not physical. Fourteen are principal nadis, of which the three most important are *ida*, *pingala* and *sushumna*. These nadis extend from the area of the female cervix or the male perineum up to the top of the spine at the back of the head behind the eyebrow centre.

Ida nadi flows from the left of the base of the body, swings in again to cross over the base of the spine at the coccyx, then continues to flow over to the right and come in again to the spine behind the navel, continues on the left side up to the centre of the chest, then flows on the right side to the base of the neck and then on the left and into the top of the spine at the level of the eyebrow centre. Pingala nadi is the mirror image of ida, and sushumna flows in the centre of the spinal column.

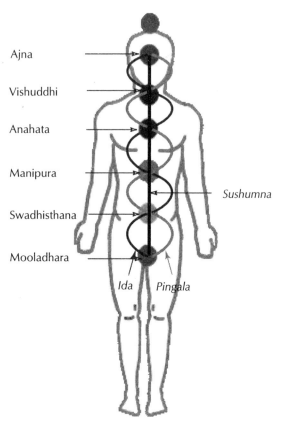

Ajna

Vishuddhi

Anahata

Manipura

Sushumna

Swadhisthana

Mooladhara

Ida   Pingala

Ida, Pingala, Sushumna and the Chakras

The chakras manifest from the flow of prana in the nadis and form at each of the points of confluence of the three main nadis (as well as the flows of thousands of others). These intricate manifold flow paths are said to awaken when the blockages are first removed and the flow is then activated. One way this can be done is through repeated performance of the appropriate capacity until it is perfected and is said to be a talent. Through lifetimes of practice of skills such as music, dancing, writing, communicating, healing and managing, we develop these skills. Actually we are developing the mental capacity so that we become talented and kundalini shakti flows to that region of the mind, and the appropriate chakra. Another way is by directly concentrating on sushumna nadi and drawing prana up from the base chakra. This is the process of awakening shakti: first the path must be purified and awakened and then shakti is free to ascend and supply the personality with energy to perform superhuman deeds.

Throughout the body these subtle chakras and nadis are described as having various colours, as seen by clairvoyants. These psychic systems have their physical manifestations in the body: ida functions through the parasympathetic nervous system and pingala through the sympathetic nervous system. The three important nadis are linked with the breath in the nostrils. When the left nostril is flowing freely, ida is functioning. In this state we are ready for mental and imaginary work – this is the moon or female aspect in us. When the right nostril is flowing pingala is functioning and we are charged with vitality and ready for action and physical work – this is the sun or male aspect in us. Ida has a cooling effect, whereas pingala has a heating effect.

Kundalini tantra explains that in the unevolved personality, shakti, the divine energy, sleeps and this dormant energy has the psychic form of a coiled serpent lying in the base chakra, mooladhara.

The chakras are connected to aspects of the personality as well as to regions of the brain. Together with the awakening of unconscious potential, prana flows along nadis to the appropriate chakra and in turn the chakra expands, giving its characteristic light and colour. Life's lessons are a gradual process of awakening kundalini in the chakras. By learning to live life simply and happily without the need for luxuries, we can overcome fear of poverty and gain security thus initiating an increased flow of prana to mooladhara chakra and the characteristic four-petalled red lotus expands. We can also use the techniques of meditation, mantra and kriya to awaken mooladhara. This will awaken the unconscious fears and insecurities, which must be dealt with so that they are expressed without judgment. This requires training,

51

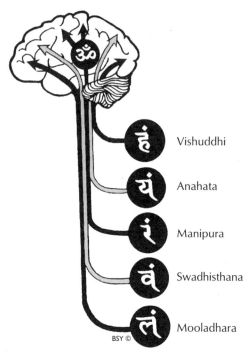

हं	Vishuddhi
यं	Anahata
रं	Manipura
वं	Swadhisthana
लं	Mooladhara

BSY ©

Arousal of Different Brain Centres

preparation and guidance from an experienced guide or
guru. Similarly, for the awakening of swadhisthana we must
live a life of selflessness and celibacy to awaken a whole
gamut of unconscious impressions to do with our emotional
needs. For manipura we must live a life of striving to develop
our will; for anahata we must expand our circle of care from
the immediate family to all those in need; and for vishuddhi
we must develop our capacity for beautiful artistic expression
through speech, word and form.

Ajna is the chakra of the mind whereas the lower chakras
are the chakras of the five elements or *panchabhootas*. These
elements are earth for mooladhara, water for swadhisthana,
fire for manipura, air for anahata and ether for vishuddhi.
Each of the chakras is a manifestation of our psychic
personality. The physical body with its organs, flesh, blood,

motor nerves and sensory nerves is composed of, and is the subsequent manifestations of, these elements. Between mooladhara and vishuddhi the whole gamut of individual experiences are stored in the mind in the form of *samskaras* or latent impressions. Through awakening of any of the lower chakras we awaken individual experiences with which we identify.

Unconscious insecurities and fears awaken through concentration on mooladhara and these are basic to the preservation of life. These fears are a driving unconscious force in life and are responsible for our extreme efforts to preserve our individual status quo, be it wealth, material standing in society, insurance for the present and plans for preservation into the future. These qualities of mind that manifest in mooladhara are basic qualities to do with material gain and consequently come under the classification of the earth element or *prithvi tattwa*.

The water element or *apas tattwa* is the classification of that area of the personality represented by swadhisthana and is the emotional aspect of mind. Purification of this portion of the personality will release unconscious traumatic or shocking experiences of the past. Concentration on manipura, anahata and vishuddhi also releases unconscious experiences that we identify with. The experiences released in each of the chakras are discussed in depth in *Kundalini Tantra* by Swami Satyananda Saraswati and in *Practical Yoga Psychology* by Dr Rishi Vivekananda. According to these authors the experiences are pleasant or unpleasant or a mixture of both.

The experiences in the lower chakras between mooladhara and vishuddhi are something that we observe happening to us. In other words they include an aspect of the experiencer; they are dualistic or include the ego and are difficult to traverse. Most unconscious experiences are unconscious because we prefer not to experience them; the pain, horror, fear, guilt or other form of rejection that we associate with those experiences means that we have suppressed the experience from coming into the light of the mind.

Awakening ajna

Awakening ajna is a mental experience beyond the ego. Swami Satyananda writes in *Kundalini Tantra*, "When the mind is concentrated at this conjunction (where ida, pingala and sushumna merge at the eyebrow centre and flow as one stream to sahasrara) transformation of individual consciousness is brought about by the merging of the three great forces. Individual consciousness is mainly comprised of ego, and it is on account of ego that we are aware of dualities. As long as there is duality there cannot be samadhi; as long as you remember yourself you cannot get out of yourself.

"Although there are experiences of trance in the other chakras, there is no merger of the individual ego with the cosmic ego. All throughout you are trying to assert yourself behind all the experiences you are having, but when ida and pingala unite with sushumna in ajna chakra, you lose yourself completely. By this I do not mean that you become unconscious; your awareness expands and becomes homogeneous. The individual awareness falls flat and you completely transcend the realm of duality. Therefore, ajna chakra is a very important centre which you must experience in order to bring about purification of the mind. Once the mind is purified, the experience and awakening of other chakras can proceed."

Manas (mind) is purified by *tapas* (austerity) and tapas is the plane or *loka* of ajna. When we reach the point in our life where there is nothing more to achieve on this worldly plane, yet we desire higher or transcendental experience, we find the highest bliss in exploring new experiences within the mind. Knowledge, ideas and visions unsupported by any external stimulus are sufficient for contentment and the preservation of this ecstatic state. Progress in opening up yet further unexplored regions of the mind is achieved by continued *sadhana,* practice, and tapasya, otherwise known as austerities or extending the limitations of human existence.

Through tapasya we raise the energetic vibration of the mind and purify the mind, igniting the fire of mental purification. The right tapasya at the right time for each individual must be carefully performed. The first rule of tapasya is that it should be joyful and not a torture, and it should bring a sense of achievement in conquering the habits and customs of ordinary human behaviour. Overcoming cold, heat, hunger and thirst are common austerities. It is difficult for the ordinary person to appreciate that suffering these can be a joy, yet there comes a time in life when it is right to perform such tapasya. The high energy state of bliss associated with this and the level of happiness and contentment is remembered long after performance of tapasya has been completed.

By performing tapas this chakra can be awakened so that the new planes and dimensions of consciousness are opened up. Ajna is spiritually, psychically and practically the most important chakra because of its overall effects on the psychic human personality. Ajna is the place where divine knowledge, knowledge of the universe, becomes known.

Psychic vision begins with a tiny internal spark or a tiny star. By holding the hands over the eyes or by simply closing the eyes and by becoming aware of the area around the eyebrow centre, sparks of light like the twinkling of stars, a large pulsating white light or a circle of coloured light can be seen. In sleep we see dreams; in meditation we see visions. Sometimes the most wonderful poetry seems to pour through the mind. When we have been working and working on a problem until completely fatigued and resigned to failure, with a flash, and with the power of the sun, the solution strikes. All these phenomena involve the function of subtle states of mind beyond the level of everyday waking consciousness. The link between our conscious self and these types of phenomena is through awakening ajna chakra.

The physical aspects of ajna chakra are the pharyngeal plexus and the pineal gland. *Ajna* means command. It is variously named *trikuti, jnana netra, bhrumadhya, triveni, mukta triveni, shiva netra* and *brahmara guha*. It is through this centre that the guru may be communicated with, and is hence often called the guru chakra; however, this is a misnomer as guru chakra is beyond ajna and will be discussed later.

Extra sensory perception phenomena are also perceived through ajna chakra. As soon as we become adept at communicating through an awakened ajna we gain the ability to influence others by our thoughts and this is where ethics and personal discipline become paramount. It is egotistically very appealing to be able to direct your own thoughts and wishes into the personality of others without their being conscious of it. We can send a wish to someone's eyebrow centre or into their drink or food without their knowledge. However, these actions do have their consequences and when someone else fulfils your wish, you are also a partner to this and you in fact become their possession to the detriment of your liberty and independence. Therefore, the intent must be beneficial, harmless and selfless to all concerned.

When the power of mind is expressed through an awakened ajna, thoughts initiate a process culminating in appropriate results, such is the power of an awakened kundalini and mind. The sankalpa in yoga nidra is just one example of this manifestation, where a thought can be translated into one's life purpose or direction, and when we are convinced something will happen, it can and does. Many have stumbled onto this fact and begin to teach others about such things as wealth creation, success and happiness through the security of knowing you can have whatever you want. Students often use affirmations or positive statements, and absorb the ideas without developing the power of mind to fulfil them. They become slaves to the techniques and to the ideals of such success.

As students of yoga we know that these efforts are not at all liberating and in fact transform life into a struggle for achievement. The outcomes for students of these harbingers of success and good fortune are tensions and worries compounded by a newly ignited hope and greed. Therefore, the wise choose to utilise their powers of mind selflessly or for the guru's mission, as the guru ensures there is no selfish reward.

It is during deep meditation on this chakra that it can be perceived in a form that various yogis have described similarly. During the practice of kundalini yoga the awakening of latent psychic energy occurs and the full glory of the colours, forms, structures and functions of the chakras is experienced together with the associated states of mind and levels of energy and perceptive abilities.

6

Ajna Chakra in the Tantras

A ccording to the tantras, ajna is the sixth chakra of the six-chakra system; however, there are more than six chakras. By including *hrit chakra* as an individual eight-petalled chakra not separate from anahata, as well as *talu chakra* above vishuddhi in the throat, ajna becomes the eighth chakra.

Tantric terms for ajna include: *ajnapatra* (ajna with petals), *ajna-pura* (ajna centre), *ajna-puri* (ajna centre), *ajnambuja* (ajna lotus), *ajna-parikaja* (-lotus), *jnana-padma* (the lotus that gives knowledge), *dwidala* (the two-petalled), *dwidalambhuja* (the two-petalled lotus), *dwidala kamala* (the two-petalled lotus), *dwipatra* (the two-petalled), *bhrusaroruha* (lotus in the eyebrow centre), *triveni kamala* (lotus at the confluence of the three nadis), *netra padma* (two-petalled lotus), *netra patra* (two-petalled), *bhru-mandala* (eyebrow abode), *bhrumadhya* (eyebrow centre), *bhrumadhyaga-padma* (chakra in the eyebrow centre), *bhrumadhya chakra* (chakra in the eyebrow centre) and *bhrumoola* (the basis of the eyebrows).

The attainment of the union called yoga by the awakening of nadis, chakras and shakti using the techniques of kundalini yoga has its most ancient origins in tantra. Many tantras reveal descriptions of the kundalini experiences of their authors. Pursuit in other paths of yoga does not preclude kundalini type experiences, rather the opposite is true.

Upanishadic seers have reported and emphasized the necessity of withdrawing the prana from the nadis of worldly existence and centralizing the flow in sushumna in order to transcend the mundane empirical experience of time and space. Various upanishads also reveal elements of the chakra system; however, the pursuit of kundalini yoga within the tantric system must have proved more efficacious as the tantras are more complete in their descriptions.

It is from these upanishadic seers that we can deduce that the pursuit of classic yoga paths such as raja yoga is also a process of kundalini yoga. Raja yoga teaches the sadhaka to sit and withdraw from the senses (pratyahara), thus introverting the awareness and pursuing an internal object or process of concentration. During this process there is a simultaneous change in the flows of prana. Most noticeably, the equalization of breath flowing in both nostrils indicates that the pranic flow is centralized in sushumna.

Kundalini yoga had remained relatively unknown other than to some Sanskrit scholars and pandits until Sir John Woodroffe, a former chief justice of Calcutta High Court, published his translation and commentary of Acharya Swami Poornananda's Sat Chakra Nirupana. Using the nom de plume Arthur Avalon, he published The Serpent Power in 1919 and today this text still stands out as a landmark volume, turning the tide of interest toward the relatively easier paths for evolution of the human personality.

Tantra had for many years suffered bad press. It had been exploited for worldly selfish gain to meet a need or hunger for greed, success, fame and lust, until Arthur Avalon's books threw light on the subjects of tantra and kundalini. Tantra was regarded as a refuge for the immoral. Publication of The Serpent Power brought respect, decency and repute, making the subject available to the West.

Today in the West, tantra and kundalini yoga are in their ascendancy. Acceptance that the Divine can have a multitude of faces and forms, including that of an increasingly popular goddess of varying forms, can be attributed to our opening new horizons in a search for divine relations with the female personification of God. This goddess is an appealing and fascinating mixture of power and knowledge capable of performing the most sublime as well as the most terrifying deeds, necessary for the growth of her followers. She is well known as Durga, Saraswati, Lakshmi and Kali, and in the context of kundalini yoga she comes in a host of names and forms.

The awakening of kundalini shakti is experienced in the form of an awakening serpent or lightning flashes in mooladhara, and this marks the beginning of the journey to limitless existence unconstrained by the dominant fears, desires and unconscious forces of the ordinary person.

Ajna is usually considered to be a single chakra; however, there are numerous references to a series of chakras, consisting of *ajna, manas, indu* and *nirvana* chakras, and then the awakening continues on to sahasrara. Initially it is very difficult to become aware of ajna chakra and so we concentrate on *ajna kshetram* (the eyebrow centre), which is directly connected to ajna chakra. That is why it has always been an Indian custom to place a coloured paste or powder there. This paste is made of varying substances, including sandalwood, chalk and one of particular interest, *sindoor*, which contains mercury. By applying sindoor to the eyebrow centre a constant pressure is exerted on the nerve that runs from the eyebrow centre *(bhrumadhya)* to the medulla oblongata at the top of the spine.

It should also be mentioned here that the pineal gland is the physical adjunct to ajna chakra, just as the pituitary gland is the physical adjunct to sahasrara chakra. Until ajna is awakened the qualities of sahasrara are dormant, and in the same way the circadian rhythms and adult sensual and sexual secretions of the pituitary gland are not secreted until the degeneration of the pineal gland in pre-pubescent years.

According to *Sat Chakra Nirupana*, ajna is symbolized by a two-petalled lotus which is white like the moon. Swami Satyananda in his book *Kundalini Tantra* adds to this by saying "according to scriptures it is a pale colour, light grey like a rainy day. Some say it is white like the moon, or silver, but actually it is an intangible colour."

60

The position of ajna is in sushumna at the level of the eyebrow centre. The two-petalled lotus has the Shakti Hakini in the pericarp of ajna and above Hakini is the *Itara lingam*, the shining black symbol of Shiva.

Sat Chakra Nirupanam

In the tantric texts much has been written about the chakras, their descriptions and the techniques used for their awakening. The following seven verses taken from the *Sat Chakra Nirupanam* (description of six chakras) give a most beautiful description of ajna chakra. *Sat Chakra Nirupanam* describes ajna as being white like the moon with even whiter letters on the petals.

In order to facilitate an initial appreciation of these seven verses, only a simple and direct translation is given here only. Please refer to the Appendix for transliteration of each verse, a more detailed translation as well as commentaries on each verse.

Verses 32–38

The ajna lotus emits a cool white light. The letters Ham (हं) and Ksham (क्षं) radiate from the two petals. It shines with the glory resultant of deepest meditation. Within is Shakti Hakini with faces like six moons. She has six arms; two portraying the freeing of fear and giving of boons, one holding a book, one a skull, one a damaru and one a japa mala. Her mind is pure.   (32)

Within the lotus is the chitta. In the central triangle are the shiva lingam and the yoni, formed by lines of flashing light. Here Om (ॐ) can be known, illuminating the chitrini nadi. The sadhaka should meditate on these with a steady heart.   (33)

The best sadhaka, who continuously meditates on this lotus, can quickly enter another's body, think perfectly and attain omniscience. He becomes an expert on the scriptures and a benefactor to all. He sees the oneness of Brahman and acquires many siddhis. He can become the master of creation, preservation and destruction.   (34)

The triangle in the middle of the chakra holds the combination of letters forming the pranava. This atman, which is buddhi, radiates like a flame. Above is the crescent moon, above this is ma-kara and above this is nada which is whiter than the moon.   (35)

Within the lotus the meditator dwells detached, as in a house hanging without support. The method is learned through service to a paramguru. When the meditation on Om (ॐ) is dissolved, he sees fiery sparks above the triangle.   (36)

Then he sees the light like a flaming lamp. It has lustre like the morning sun, shining between mooladhara and sahasrara and throughout the whole universe. Here Bhagavan manifests all His might. He is the permanent and omniscient witness, residing here in the region of fire, moon and sun.   (37)

This is the blissful abode of Vishnu. At the time of death the perfect yogi places his prana here. After death he enters the blissful, eternal primeval deva, the purusha, who is known in the vedas.   (38)

7

Psycho-Physiological Aspects

The pineal gland is the physical concomitant of ajna chakra. With ajna awakening comes the dawning of control over the effects of the lower chakras on the mind. There is a parallel here with the function of the pineal gland – the pineal acts to limit the stimulating effect of other hormones (including those related to all other chakras, including sahasrara), thus mirroring ajna's impact on the mind.

For more than 2,000 years the pineal gland has been the subject of intense philosophical speculation. It has often been described as the receiver of subtle vibrations and telepathic phenomena. Now, however, in the light of the most recent medical discoveries, there is little doubt about the role the pineal gland plays in the psychic faculties of man.

In the middle of the nineteenth century, as the sub-continent of Australia and its surrounding territory came to be explored, there was a flurry of interest centred upon a lizard native to the area, the tuatara (sphenodon punctatum). This animal is related to the extinct dinosaurs that once roamed the ancient continent of Gondawana when Australia, New Zealand, the Indonesian archipelago and Tasmania were all one land, and has survived on a few remote islands near New Zealand.

The tuatara is known for a perfectly formed third eye in the middle of its head. In addition to two ordinary eyes located on either side of its head, the third eye buried in the skull was revealed through an aperture in the bone, covered by a transparent membrane, and surrounded by a rosette of scales. It was unmistakeably a third eye, and upon dissection contained all the anatomical parts of an eye, including the lens and retina, yet did not function as an organ of sight. Another remarkable fact is that this lizard did not reproduce before twenty years of age and the male of the species did not have a penis.

Contemporary students, keen for mainstream science to verify their spiritual convictions, may leap at the speculation that this unusually developed ancient pineal is a feature of ancient civilizations based on wisdom and inner knowledge. They may also note the coincidence of total control over sexual drives being a characteristic of high levels of melatonin production, the hormone produced by the pineal. However, this has not been verified at present.

The presence of this eye in the tuatara still poses a puzzle to present-day evolutionists; almost all vertebrates possess a similar structure in the centre of their skull. It is present in many fish, all reptiles, birds and mammals, including man. Of all the organs in the body, no other organ has been subject to as many changes and developments in the course of evolution as the pineal gland. Research on fossils reveals that it acted as a third physical eye, which was sensitive to light and dark. This is evident in extinct species such as the brontosaurus and other ancient amphibian vertebrates.

Even in animals today, such as the frog, the pineal gland senses light. In the course of evolution from reptiles to birds to animals and finally to man, the eight sensory cells of the pineal have been replaced by a much more functionally intricate cell (parenchyma cell). In the highest vertebrates, such as man, no light receptive cells remain in the pineal gland, yet the function of the pineal is sensitive to the rising and setting of the sun.

Pineal gland and hormone production

For some time it has been known that the production of pineal hormones, such as melatonin, increases after dark and production peaks between midnight and brahmamuhurta (two hours before sunrise). The daily commencement and cessation of hormone production at times linked to the movement of the sun is termed circadian rhythm. Amongst yogis and meditation practitioners, brahmamuhurta has long been recognized as the preferred time for meditation, and so the concurrence of peak flows of melatonin at the preferred time of meditation is not a surprise.

The pineal is situated in the epithalamus at the centre of the brain and receives sympathetic enervation from the superior cervical ganglia via the conarian nerves. Simply put, the pineal gland is found buried nearly in the centre of the brain of any mammal. It is a white structure shaped like a pine cone. In man it is roughly a quarter of an inch long and weights about 100 milligrams. It is the only unpaired organ in the brain. After puberty this gland hardens by a process of calcification, which does not affect its functioning.

Early scientists found that young boys with tumours around the pineal gland exhibited precocious growth of the genital organs, whereas boys with pineal tumours showed delayed development of puberty characteristics. This is because the pineal gland's function is inhibited by tumours around it, but when the gland itself is tumoral, it is overactive and thus delays pubic growth. Julius Axelrod, a world-renowned biochemist, has shown in the laboratory that the pineal gland is a sensitive biological clock, which uses daily rhythms of nervous energy to stimulate endocrinal secretions. This pineal stimulating nervous activity is generated by light.

Additionally, he has discovered that the pineal gland produces the hormone melatonin, which is not produced by any other physical organ. He notes that melatonin decreases the size of the ovaries in women and increases the length of the menstrual cycle. Generally speaking, it depresses the

65

sexual function in man. It is not connected to the brain but to the sympathetic nervous system.

In darkness, the pineal gland produces melatonin only. After six hours of darkness the size of the pineal gland increases and it is activated into the production of melatonin. When light returns, the melatonin production falls off. This is similar to the function of the pituitary gland which produces ACTH (adrenocorticotrophic hormone), a supra-renal gland activator, between the hours of 3.00 am and 6.00 am. The pineal gland, which in modern times has ceased functioning as a light-sensing organ, is now controlled by light and darkness through the eyes, which affect the sympathetic nervous system, which in turn activates or deactivates the pineal gland.

In addition the pineal gland has been found to synthesize another hormone called serotonin. This hormone is produced during conditions of light. Under conditions of constant light the pineal gland ceases to produce melatonin and consistently produces large quantities of serotonin. In constant darkness, such as a darkened room, serotonin production continues at its maximum in the daytime and its minimum in the night, even though for the whole time it is dark. Furthermore, it has been found that removing the eyes of rats or severing the sympathetic nervous system has the same effect as plunging the rat into constant darkness. The daily rhythm of serotonin production continues normally under these conditions.

The daily light cycle also plays an important part in the glandular cycles of many lower animals. The increase of sunlight during springtime triggers the gonadal growth and breeding cycles of many birds and mammals which breed yearly. The daily cycle of light and darkness synchronizes a variety of daily rhythms in mammals such as the cycle of adrenal sex steroid secretions. This correlates with the sun-moon theory in yoga philosophy: the centre of the moon is ajna and the centre of the sun is manipura. These chakras correspond to the physical pineal and adrenal glands respectively.

Effects of meditation

It is believed by many experienced practitioners of meditation that the pineal gland and the higher nervous system with which it is intimately connected go through a functional change after long-term practice of meditation. This has been recently borne out by scientific investigators doing research on the electrical impulses of the brain. They have found that when a person is in an ordinary waking conscious state, the electrical waves, known as beta waves, produced by the cerebral cortex of the brain are characteristically small and rapid. When he closes his eyes, however, and maintains a relaxed but aware state of mind as is done through the yoga practices of japa and antar mouna, there is an immediate change in these wave formations, which become larger and slower. These waves are known as alpha waves and their presence has been noted in both beginners and advanced practitioners of meditation.

Yogis, Zen Buddhist monks and other experienced meditators have been found to experience an even larger, slower type of wave which is called the theta wave. It is interesting to note that these theta waves are normally found only in epileptics at the time when they are having grande mal seizures. One possible explanation for this is that when there are epileptic fits, the lower nervous system takes over complete control of the body, and the higher mind remains completely relaxed, as it is during states of deep meditation.

The state of meditation also brings about many other physiological changes which are measured side by side with the EEG brain wave measurements. The influence of a state of meditational consciousness emitting alpha waves is to lower the heartbeat, decrease oxygen consumption by the body cells, reduce carbon dioxide elimination, slow down metabolism and relax the activity of the sympathetic nervous system. The blood lactate falls most dramatically, and this is characteristically high in people suffering from nervous tension and neurosis. In meditation, that is, in the state during which the mind emits alpha waves, a process which opposes the

67

mechanisms of the adrenaline secretory system comes about. This enables the body to operate in a less tense manner.

Another group of researchers have been investigating psychic phenomena in man, particularly the relationship between extra sensory perception and alpha wave activity. An experiment was run where many people had to guess which card was inside a closed box. Psychologists found, using statistical tests, that when a person closes his eyes and concentrates on any object his alpha waves increase, and those people who emit more alpha waves were able to recognize, more often, the cards inside the box. When alpha wave emission was low, however, as it is normally with many people or when the eyes are opened, the card guessing was just chance.

The subjects of the experiment described their state of mind when alpha activity was predominant. They all agreed that it was a rather pleasant feeling with the mind vacant and they experienced an attitude of separation from the surroundings. When the subjects happened to open their eyes under these conditions they could see that environmental objects were disconnected from themselves. This describes the yogic meditational state of *pratyahara* or sense withdrawal, and the increase in the psychic capacities shown under these conditions correlates with the capacities of a person who has awakened ajna, who has the capacity to see distant objects with his divine third eye.

The panacea for most modern diseases is the alpha brain wave, which restores the body and mind to a peaceful condition and opposes the anachronistic emergency reactions which are still going on in our bodies. In the modern society, life is no more subjected to attack by wild animals or by savage tribes; however, the ancient adrenaline secretory mechanism which guards the body against such emergencies reacts to modern dangers in the same old way.

Today, man's dangers are usually in the form of fear of financial crisis, fear of loss of position and family troubles etc. Though these tensions of modern society are unreal dangers to life, to the tense mind they appear to be real. As these modern day dangers are limitless and never ending many people's bodies react continuously, and in so doing drain energy, pipe up tensions and cause physiological and mental diseases. In addition, through over use, man's greatest defence mechanism is becoming worn out, and many people find themselves unable to cope when a really dangerous situation occurs. This fact is evident from the rising number of victims of shock brought about by having to suddenly face truly dangerous, unaccustomed situations. What the doctors and scientists are now saying is that meditation is the only cure for these conditions.

From ancient times, rishis, munis and yogis have been saying that meditation leads to peace of mind, and it has always been associated with the spiritual quest. Yogis, who are scientists of the subtle mind, have always spoken of telepathy as a *siddhi*, a psychic power for thought com-munication and clairaudience. The medium of such siddhis is ajna, and its physical terminus is the pineal gland, which is connected to the brain.

It has been stated by great yogis such as Swami Sivananda that the pineal gland is the receptor and sender of the subtle vibrations which carry thoughts and psychic phenomena throughout the cosmos. The pineal gland converts brain waves into subtle electrical signals travelling faster than the speed of light, which are stored in the individual brain. Persons who have developed such faculties as subtle hearing and sight have done so by virtue of ajna's transmutation of their increased alpha wave activity.

Modern man is intellectual and prefers to base his life on scientific facts rather than beliefs in ancient culture, ancient scriptures and teachings by pandits, monks, rabbis and priests of religions. Today, the only accepted fact is a scientific fact, and the scientific experiment described earlier proves that it is not coincidence but actual fact that some people, who have a meditative mind, whose brain waves are predominantly alpha, can predict and have knowledge of outer and inner events which are beyond the reach of the senses.

The psychic powers which so many people strive to attain through the various practices of meditation such as mantra repetition and other types of sadhana are the very first signs of a spiritual aspirant moving on the path. Although the pure spiritual aspirant denies himself the use of these powers, lest they lead to his downfall, these inner faculties are in each and every one of us. We only have to do the practices for awakening the higher centres in the brain which are associated with ajna in order to open these doorways to new experiences.

Thus, ajna and the pineal gland act as the channels through which the subtle vibrations are sent out into the cosmos, or are received. Ajna is the best known and most respected chakra; it has always been held in high esteem and probably the best known practices of meditation are designed to awaken ajna and increase the activity of the pineal gland. Persons who enjoy excessive sexual stimulation will have more difficulty in attaining siddhis and may have trouble in maintaining the siddhis they have attained. This fact is well known amongst all spiritual aspirants and is in harmony with the effect of the pineal gland regulating the activity of the sexual function.

However, nothing in life is absolute and sexual abstinence for those idealists who are not sufficiently pure may actually be more harmful than helpful in their progress in meditation. Often such aspirants find the effort required to halt sexual activity to be so difficult or indeed impossible that understandable lapses occur yet are fraught with tensions and guilt. Therefore, one should abstain when abstinence would not be a struggle.

Research on the pineal gland

Serena Roney-Dougal is a parapsychologist who has written many papers on the function of the pineal gland in the chakra system. A three part series, 'On a Possible Psychophysiology of the Yogic Chakra System' was republished in the Sivananda Math journal, *YOGA* (May, July, September

2000). Her work validates the role of melatonin during meditative states.

Roney-Dougal writes that the main function of the pineal gland is to make neuro-hormones, which affect both the brain and the body. The pineal works with the pituitary through the hypothalamus, controlling the endocrine system. It is one of the regulators of our circadian rhythm, is implicated in our emotional state, reproductive function, possibly dream sleep and in certain psychoses. Melatonin is the best studied of the pineal neuro-hormones and was first isolated from cattle in 1963. Before this the pineal was generally considered in the West to be vestigial. Amphibians and reptiles have light sensitive cells in the pineal gland, which for them is literally a light sensitive third eye at the top of the brain. In humans, fibres from the inferior accessory optic tract go to the pineal; these are separate from the main optic tract bundle, which suggests that the light sensitivity of the pineal is not necessarily related to sight (Eichler, 1985).

The pineal gland is shaped like a tiny pinecone and is thus aptly named. Older texts describe this vestigial organ as a relic from our reptilian past. Serena Roney-Dougal is unique in her description of the physical aspects of ajna as a bilobed (two lobes or two petals) and a joining of the two glands, pituitary and pineal; the established system is to ascribe the physical concomitant of sahasrara to the pituitary and that of ajna to the pineal.

Most people have heard of the pituitary gland, often known as the 'master gland' in that the hormones it makes exert a controlling effect on the endocrine organs. We can think of the pituitary as being an 'on switch' and the pineal as being an 'off switch' (the mistress gland) in that it works with the pituitary by switching off the endocrine organs.

The form of ajna is traditionally depicted as bilobed and we can understand this to be the joining of the two glands, pituitary and pineal, which makes very good sense from a neuro-endocrinological point of view. This makes much better sense than assigning the pituitary to sahasrara, the crown

chakra, as some systems do, since sahasrara is better understood as the culmination of everything, the whole rather
than any of the parts. Just as mooladhara is considered to be
the top chakra of animals and the bottom of humans, so
sahasrara can be understood as the top chakra of humanity
and the bottom chakra of the divine order of being.

There is a large body of scientific evidence suggesting that
the pineal gland produces a chemical in the brain that enhances
psychic paranormal or meditative states. Roney-Dougal says,
"Neurochemical and anthropological evidence suggests that
the pineal gland may produce a neuro-modulator that
enhances a psi-conducive state of consciousness." An abstract
of this research was presented at the Parapsychological
Association Convention in 1985 (Roney-Dougal, 1986). For
full details of this research see Roney-Dougal (1988, 1989,
1990, 1991, 1993). In brief, the pineal gland has been found
to synthesize various beta-carbolines and peptides, and to
contain enzymes that produce psycho-active compounds such
as 5-methoxy dimethyltryptamine (5MeODMT). "The two
precursors that are most likely to be involved in the synthesis
of such compounds are serotonin (5-hydroxytryptamine, 5HT)
and tryptamine. These have wide-ranging effects throughout
our brain and body, affecting the gonads, adrenals, pancreas,
thyroid, and other emotional and endocrine activities."
(Strassman, 1990)

At this stage of the discussion it is appropriate to view a
historical perspective on the development of scientific
knowledge of the functioning of the pineal gland. It was first
found that melatonin was a hormone manufactured by the
pineal gland in 1959 by Dr Aaron Lerner at Yale University.
He concluded that melatonin must have been the result of
the reaction of certain enzymes upon serotonin, which must
have pre-existed in the pineal gland. Serotonin is not an
unusual chemical in nature; it is found in many places,
including plants such as bananas, figs and plums.

Professor E.J. Gaddum at the University of Edinburgh was
the first to note a connection between serotonin and mental

states of being. In a paper published in 1953 he pointed out that LSD-25 was a potent antagonist to serotonin. LSD-25 was said to be the drug for altering the mind and inducing mental states free from the mentally limiting encumbrance of social and environmental patterns. The experience was termed transcendental and likened to the death of the ego as portrayed by Dr Timothy Leary and others who were the leaders of the 'hippy culture' of the 1970s.

Subsequently, it was found that LSD occupies serotonin receptor sites, for a brief time suppressing the action of serotonin. This is followed by a surge in serotonin concentrations, giving rise to the so-called LSD experience, which is the psi experience. This is in agreement with the reported experience some 20–30 minutes after ingesting LSD. The initial 'high' is reported to be peaceful, totally relaxed as if bathed in golden light and certainly out of this world, and is followed by a trip through the unconscious with a myriad of patterns and images. The LSD practitioner is likely to experience the ordinary mind of everyday humdrum conditioned existence as something shallow, unreal and separate from them, and with this there is the realization that within lies a glorious and deep existence, which is the truth. From this the alternative hippy culture sprang and many among their ranks took to spiritual disciplines so that the experience of the truth could live with them.

Julius Axelrod has studied the roles of melatonin and its precursor serotonin, and found that melatonin suppresses physiological sexuality in mammals. Test animals were stimulated to manufacture excessive amounts of melatonin, which resulted in their gonads and ovaries shrinking, atrophying. The oestrous or fertility cycle in females could likewise be altered experimentally by doses of melatonin.

Axelrod also discovered that the pineal gland produces chemicals to a circadian rhythm; by altering light conditions he could extend, contract, or even stabilize the chemical production rhythms of the pineal. So the pineal gland research to date has uncovered three basic points:

1. The pineal produces melatonin, which is associated with the internal unconscious and subconscious experiences similar to the experiences of meditation.
2. Melatonin suppresses sexuality and the functionality of the sexual organs, creating a balance with the sexually stimulating effect of other hormones and of external conscious or worldly life. The literature of religious mysticism in all ages and all societies has viewed carnal passion as the antagonist of the ecstasy of spiritual experience.
3. The production of melatonin is regulated by light; in the absence of light at night production is at its highest.

The fact that the pineal responds to light, even if this response is indirect via the central nervous system, has some fascinating and far-reaching conceptual applications. There are many behavioural changes which overtake animals as the seasons change, and which can be produced out of season in the laboratory by simulating the appropriate span of artificial daylight. This poses the question, "Do such seasonal changes in mood and behaviour persist in humans?"

Greg Tooley is a researcher on the effects of meditation on melatonin levels in the blood. He works at the School of Psychology, La Trobe University, Bundoora, Victoria, Australia. During the proceedings of the 1996 World Yoga Convention held in Sydney, he reported that his research showed that:
- Melatonin production peaked at around midnight.
- The production level of melatonin increases with the number of years of meditation practice of each subject.

In a subsequent research paper (G.A. Tooley et al, 2000, *Biological Psychology*, 53, 69–78, 71), Tooley describes some of the health benefits of melatonin and reports on previous research (Panzer and Viljoen, 1997), on immunoaugmentation (Maestroni et al, 1986), and anti-ageing (Maestroni et al, 1989):

"Although these properties have not yet been clearly established in humans, the fact that melatonin has been found to be an extremely potent antioxidant and free-radical scavenger (Reiter et al, 1997) suggests that it may have an important role in reducing the cellular damage associated with the wear and tear of normal day to day life. In this context it is interesting to note that anti-cancer (Solberg et al, 1995; Meares, 1979), immunoaugmenting (Wallace, 1989), anti-ageing (Wallace et al,1982) and anti-stress (Jevning et al, 1978a,b; MacLean et al, 1997) properties have also been claimed in relation to meditation. While the validity of the anti-cancer and anti-ageing claims in particular are debatable, the parallels with those made for melatonin are intriguing, and invite speculation that one of the mechanisms by which meditation might achieve some of its health benefits may be through an effect on circulating melatonin levels. With the above in mind, the following investigations were undertaken in order to test whether a period of meditation could acutely affect plasma melatonin levels."

In simple language this means that melatonin has the effect of anti-ageing, anti-stress, boosting the immune system and can be helpful in the treatment of cancer as well as repairing the cellular damage caused by the stresses and strains of worldly life. These benefits run parallel to the benefits of meditation and replicate the conclusions drawn in a much earlier book by Herbert Benson titled *Relaxation Response*. In this book the effects of meditation were measured by fourteen physiological functions such as heart rate, blood pressure, lactic acid content, electrical conductivity of the skin, etc. At the time of the book (1976) the benefits of melatonin were not known; however, the benefits of meditation were just starting to come into the view of medical research.

8

Psychic and Mystic Concepts

In recent years it has come to light that about one person in fifty cannot recall faces. Often if a person changes clothes, pulls their hair back or puts a hat on, they become unrecognizable to those who suffer from this problem. Research has revealed that such people do not look at the eyebrow centre when trying to recognize people. Further it has been found that by training people to concentrate on the eyebrow centre, the incapacity diminishes remarkably. One can now speculate whether it is the features we recognize or whether we connect more subtle features through ajna.

Ajna is the command centre of the psychic body and it lies in the exact centre of the brain. It is most readily perceived directly behind the eyebrow centre in the region of the frontal sinuses, and its second centre of perception is in the medulla oblongata at the top of the spinal column. Sahasrara lies in the metacortex, or higher brain. Connecting these two centres is the *mahanada*, which arises out of the dissolution of the three nadis: *ida, pingala* and *sushumna*, through which subtle currents flow. When a sadhaka enters into meditation, the force of willpower brings the subtle energies into motion and when contacted with the mind's awareness, they appear in the form of light.

This light in meditation is first seen in a circular form and sometimes like the flame of a candle and is a sign of the aspirant advancing on the path. Often people interpret the vision of light in ajna as a very significant sign, bestowing wisdom, knowledge, bliss and greatness; but this interpretation is incorrect. The true light of knowledge, called *samadhi*, is beyond all experience. It is of the highest spiritual order and is the aim of all true yogis. In this state there is no beginning or end, just infinite truth, consciousness and bliss. The light of ajna, however, is an experience that marks the beginning of psychic life, and the light of knowledge, once dawned, is an experience from which there is no return. When it comes about, the sadhaka is advised to practise meditation, with awareness on this point, until his consciousness merges with the light.

The more accomplished sadhaka often sees the two charged particles of ajna as two petals of the ajna *padma* (lotus). The reason for the appearance of the two petals surrounding a circular form is that this chakra is the meeting point of the three principal nadis: ida, pingala and sushumna. These three nadis terminate near the *brahmarandhra* at the top of the skull, a little above ajna.

Nadis and prana

These nadis are the psychic equivalents of the sympathetic (SNS) and parasympathetic (PNS) nervous systems, which control all the involuntary functions such as heartbeat, digestion, glandular secretion and peristalsis. In general the PNS is the inhibitor of these functions, slowing down metabolism, and the SNS is the stimulator, speeding these functions up. When a greater amount of air flows through the right nostril, pingala tends to be stimulated. This has a heating effect on the body, with the SNS speeding up metabolism. When more air flows through the left nostril, ida tends to be stimulated with a resultant cooling effect and metabolic slowdown.

Pingala is related to the physical aspect of existence and ida to the mental aspect. In most people there is a daily cycle of alternate stimulation of ida and pingala, with each cycle lasting anywhere between one and four hours. In well-balanced individuals there is an equal flow in both during a day and the changes correspond to daily cycles of moods and activities. Sick or mentally disturbed persons generally have this system out of balance, as can be noted in the case of high-strung neurotics whose right nostrils are always more open, or of severely depressed persons whose left nostrils tend to flow.

The connecting link between the breath, the mind and the psychic body is the olfactory bulb and the limbic formation of the brain, which is connected to the pineal gland. This olfactory bulb, which is also the organ of smell, senses which nostril is flowing and relays this information to the rest of the brain. It is a very complex organ, with thousands of nerve connections leading to all parts of the nervous system, for which neurologists cannot find any functional purpose. It has two lobes, one directly over each nostril.

The science of swara yoga deals directly with this alternating flow of forces. In its practice the flow is noted by the aspirant, who is able to balance it or change it from ida to pingala or vice versa, often by exerting physical pressure at a point directly below the armpit. This is often done in conjunction with pranayama practices in which the breath alternates between the two nostrils in certain prescribed ratios based on the time unit (*matra*) of approximately one second. An advanced example of a pranayama ratio is given in chapter 9.

It is through these nadis that the prana can be drawn up from manipura to ajna and then distributed to any part of the body or to other bodies. It is through them that the vital energy flows, which is so necessary for mental and physical work. Through the practices of pranayama and ajapa japa these nadis are purified and prana flows easily. By virtue of special sadhanas, spiritual aspirants can awaken prana shakti in the body and it is on this energy alone that they can find strength to combat disease, to live on poor diets, to maintain long hours of sadhana and to work hard for years and years without a rest.

Yogis who have tapped this source of energy never suffer from a lack of it and perform miraculous feats of healing. Their work and efforts are selfless; it is all for others. Their tireless efforts, involving continual mental and physical selfless work for the whole of their very long lives, ensure expansion in every aspect of their being. Sadhana and service is the way to expand out of the limited self to the unlimited selfless self.

The energy that lifts the jumbo jet into the air, the energy we use to carry loads, the energy to move stool through the intestines, to inhale and exhale, or to pump blood around the body is all the same energy. This energy is prana. Mind is the controller of prana, body is the motor and prana is its driving force.

The prana in the body is stored in manipura and the seat of the cosmic mind is ajna. In psychic healing processes, prana is drawn up from manipura to ajna and then directed to the required point. It is through the power of will that the mind has the capacity to direct the prana. The prana store is always replenished by an involuntary and spontaneous process. As prana is connected with the sun and mind with the moon, action on the physical plane which functions under volition is lunar and action which functions reflexively is solar.

Nectar of immortality

Sun is said to be in the navel region, with face downwards, emitting poisons leading to mortality. By yoga practices we come to discover a flower in the throat (vishuddhi) and this flower can be turned upward to emit *soma*, the nectar of immortality. Soma rises up to ajna, the seat of the moon, where it is converted into astral fluid.

This is described in the *Yoga Shikha Upanishad* (5:32–33): "The potential energy of the universe is the energy which has its aspect in man. The fire in the sky, which is the sun, corresponds to the fire in the navel region of man. In the navel the sun is poison, but when it is directed upwards, it begins to produce nectar. The moon is at the root of the palate, which drops nectar downwards."

Further, in *Gheranda Samhita* (3:28–31) it is said: "Sun is located in the root of the navel and moon is located in the root of the palate. The nectar coming out of the moon is absorbed by the sun and so do men die. Direct the sun upwards and bring the moon downwards. This is vipareeta karani mudra, the secret of all tantras. Place the head on the ground along with both the arms. Direct the legs upward keeping the head fixed on the floor. It is vipareeta karani mudra as opined by the yogins. Daily practice of vipareeta karani mudra keeps death and old age away, and even disturbances of nature never affect him. He becomes a siddha of all worlds."

The physical secretions of the thyroid, pituitary, pineal and adrenal glands are controlled through this practice. Soma is the most precious bodily product and yogis practise khechari mudra as well as vipareeta karani mudra in order to preserve the secretion. Yogis, who make the fluid drop down the nasal roof by raising the tongue in the palatal cavity above the soft palate, thus tasting it, are immune to poisons and snake bites. Soma is usually referred to as amrit and *amrit* is translated as nectar of immortality. A direct translation is 'not mortal', meaning immortal.

Actually the moon centre is above the palate, which corresponds to the physiological site of the glands. The secretion coming out of the palatal gland is absorbed and dried by the heat of the glands in the lower region. If the secretion coming out of the palate is preserved somehow, the tissues of the body will not undergo a speedy decay.

Mind, soma and astral fluid are all associated with the moon centre of ajna. Soma and astral fluid give strength to the mind; this strength is required for bearing the austerities of spiritual life. By conversion of the precious fluids from manipura into soma, the nectar can be tasted in the back of the mouth from the root of the palate. This effect changes the entire structure of the body. Many yogis who have perfected this practice reach very high levels of consciousness, attain many siddhis and live very long. They enjoy perfect health and great strength to bear and enjoy the severe austerities of ascetic life. These yogis often live high in the mountains, under severe conditions of cold without clothing, living quarters or fire for warmth, eating only two or three rotis (round flat bread) and some dal and water daily. Many yogis living in isolation, under these conditions, have reached ages of 200 and 300 years.

Power of ajna

These practices that preserve the secretion of soma are difficult to perfect quickly and must be practised regularly over a period of time in order to achieve perfection. These practices must be done in conjunction with other kinds of sadhana. The combined effect of these sadhanas will keep the mind fresh and alert so that much energy can be directed towards ajna. The awakened chakra supplements the other sadhanas; the mental power of such a mind is great, and progress in sadhana is fast. The light of ajna is awakened and burns with increasing brilliance until it acquires the brilliance of a thousand suns.

The white light of ajna is infinitely powerful. By force of will one can take one's consciousness to distant places and thus obtain knowledge of other objects. This is the divine light through which religious seekers see visions of their God. By awakening ajna the actual form of the astral bodies can be perceived. Telepathy, clairvoyance, clairaudience and intuition all function through this chakra. By meditation on ajna one gets the siddhis to satisfy any desire and the command made through ajna must be fulfilled. For this reason it is called *ajna*, meaning command.

The light arising from ajna during meditation, which arises from the power of mind, is known as *prana loka*. Simultaneously, will arises from chitta and enters the intellect and the desire for knowledge follows. Thus, from ajna, will sends its vibrations out into the cosmos and comes into contact with the required object, giving satisfaction to the desire through ajna. This is the power of positive thinking

81

and the postulation of a principle that 'thoughts create things' – the universe will surely reward you in harmony with your own will. Those who have opened this passage by awakening ajna and combine this with a trained mind will achieve great deeds and are recognized as truly great people who can build missions or even empires.

Ajna is the channel of *sankalpa shakti*, power of resolution. Here yogis make their sankalpa and achieve their aims; great yogis can give blessings to humanity, send out messages for universal peace and goodwill. Their success is not born out of extraordinarily strong willpower, but because ajna is awakened, offering a channel for the will to operate throughout the universe.

This power can be used destructively as well as creatively. The performance of many of the black tantric rituals can bring sickness, death, destruction of crops due to floods or hailstorms, financial ruin and so on. This is the same power that operates through ajna.

Pineal gland

Early research on the pineal gland in man showed that the pineal cells were ocular in nature. As man evolved, the third eye ceased to function as a physical eye and the brain developed around it. Early man was not intellectually developed and his livelihood depended mainly on instinct and intuition, both of which operate through ajna. The pineal gland is connected with the SNS, which controlled most of early man's movements, as his central nervous system (CNS) had not been adequately developed. Thus the SNS and the life of early man were largely affected by surgings of the astral body. As man evolved, the functions of the SNS become subordinate and the CNS developed. In this way the astral body became subordinate, although it still continues to function by sending its impulses through the physical terminal of the pineal gland into the brain.

Modern man can now, with his well-proportioned brain and evolved state, be ready to take advantage of the astral knowledge. Because the intellectual processes and the CNS became dominant, the psychic functioning of man suffered, or underwent a process of involution.

The pineal gland serves as a physical organ for the transmission of thought form from one brain to another or from higher levels to the brain. But the awareness of this knowledge and the awareness of its mode of communication is often lacking, because most people are not aware of these higher levels of consciousness and their faculties are engaged with mental processes and emotions. Many people are sensitive to the phenomena of higher planes, but their lack of awareness is due to the absence of the connecting links with the SNS. A person may be awake on the astral plane and functioning actively thereon, but if the connections between the physical and the astral systems have not been made, there is a break in consciousness. However vivid may be the consciousness on the astral plane it cannot, until the links are functioning, bring through and impress on the physical brain the memory of higher consciousness experiences.

The evidence of the third eye used as a psychic eye is not rare, but is universally accepted by most cultures ancient and modern. Most prominent significance must be attributed to Hindus who perform a ritual, at least once a day, which includes placing a spot of coloured powder *(tilaka)* at the eyebrow centre. Many Hindu women wear this mark to indicate marriage. Hindu sadhus often mark their eyebrow centre with the trident of Lord Shiva, indicating that this is the place of confluence of the three great energies, ida, pingala and sushumna, and the home of Shiva, the symbol of cosmic consciousness in man. Ajna is the *trikuti* (e.g. the meeting point of three lines) of Ganga, Yamuna and Saraswati, three sacred rivers in India, symbolic of ida, pingala and sushumna.

When Roman Catholics genuflect before the cross, they make the sign of the cross with their fingers; the top of the cross is at ajna. Buddhists signify their reverence to ajna by placing a precious jewel or ornament at the eyebrow centre on statues of Lord Buddha. The intricate arrangement of head-dress worn by the American Indians consists of multi-coloured feathers attached to an ornamented headband. The arrangement and ornamentation of the band is symmetric above the eyebrow centre. Those members of the community who develop greater psychic faculties are entitled to wear larger head-dresses with more dazzling arrangements. The colours represent the aura that emanates from this chakra. The ancient Egyptian head-dress has an upraised serpent at the site of the eyebrow centre. The serpent itself has a spiritual significance, which is emphasized by its position.

Correlations between psychology and yoga

According to yogis, the ability to have knowledge about objects that cannot usually be perceived is a siddhi and indeed, not only yogis but also many people are capable of extra sensory perception (ESP). Many people have dreams about future events in their life and pick up the thoughts of those around them or, from their unconscious higher selves, receive messages of philosophical or spiritual content which, at the time of receiving, are pregnant with deeper meaning.

Many people are highly intuitive by way of intuitive flashes coming across the mind or, without thinking, by automatically doing the right thing at the right time. The yogi has not developed his science so that he can explore and develop these psychic phenomena, but rather, so that he can systematically and accurately gain the scientific knowledge of body and mind, a necessary precursor for a higher life.

Alpha wave predominance in the brain relates to the ESP capacity of the individual. During meditation the mind is turned inward away from the senses and the sense objects, and a state of tranquillity is reached where the mind is relaxed and its attention is fixed on an internal object. By pursuing this practice the scope of the mind expands beyond the physical barriers, its power or radiations are channelled through ajna and supersensory knowledge comes to the mind of the practitioner.

Scientists have used delicate electronic instruments to measure the conditions of meditation on ESP, whereas yogis have developed and refined their own mental capacities, and are thus able to experience and observe the same conditions for meditation on ESP. The only difference between the scientific and yogic points of view is the terminology.

The solar plexus is thus named because this centre is responsible for heat in the body. It is through this plexus in the autonomic nervous system (ANS) that the digestive process is stimulated. The SNS (pingala) and PNS (ida) meet in the eyebrow centre and flow out through the nostrils. When the right nostril is flowing, pingala is flowing and the physical or masculine aspect of man is functioning. The common characteristic of the physical aspect is action. For digestion, excretion, hard physical effort and rapid heartbeat, pingala nadi gives best efficiency whereas to attempt meditation under these conditions is extremely difficult. On the other hand, when the left nostril is flowing, ida is flowing, the female aspect of life is predominant and meditation or mental activities are preferred.

When we are agitated, excited or in a state of fear, adrenaline is pumped into the bloodstream, increasing the heartbeat, breathing rate, and in general creating great physical strength, tension and instinctive reactions to situations. This is the 'poison' which many people constantly run their lives on. Always seeking thrills and excitement, always fearing the possible losses and defeats in life, they have no time for a mental life or for meditational practices. This 'poison', recorded in scriptures 5,000 years ago, is modern man's number one killer and is the root cause of heart attack.

The adrenaline system functioned in early man on an instinctive level so that when his life was being threatened, he had this speedy secretion of adrenaline hormone to give him the necessary strength to fight or flee. In modern society, such threats are an anachronism. However, man is so attached to the symbols of his status within society that any threat to his position can set the adrenaline pumping into his blood stream for weeks and months at a time. On the short term basis, this state of tension produces toxins in the body, and the need for frequent release of tension and removal of toxins is marked by the necessity of modern man to have frequent sexual intercourse.

The characteristics of soma are the exact opposite to that of adrenaline; it has the characteristic of the moon, the mental or cooling aspect. It has been described how, through the practices of yoga, the poisons going into the body may be averted and the astral fluid may be converted into mind-stuff. Actually there is no scientific evidence for the presence of soma; however, the carefully measured physiological changes brought about by meditation and certain asanas that have been studied in detail show that the bodily changes tend toward moon characteristics in humans and exactly counter the effects of the adrenaline system. In yoga, this cooling condition is created by moving the prana from its central storehouse at manipura to ajna, where it is turned into mental energy. The techniques will be described in chapter 9.

This is why millions of people all around the world are finding a new pleasure in freedom from disease and relaxation of mental and physical tensions by the practice of yoga. In order to ensure good health modern man does not have to give up his work, his business and seek a peaceful life in health resorts, forests and lovely places. With this latest knowledge of yoga he can confidently, with a few simple daily practices, offset the tension of apparent threats which buffet him every day.

Brahmamuhurta

Brahmamuhurta is that time in the early morning, which is best for yoga practices. It is a Sanskrit word meaning the important time for Brahman. *Brahman* refers to the highest cosmic consciousness, which is that all pervading awareness to which all beings are evolving either consciously or unconsciously – that infinite all pervading consciousness that is the same within and without every being and everything. Yoga practices are designed to raise man's consciousness above the world so that he can transcend this objective universe and his mind can remain within his subtle spheres of consciousness. *Muhurta* means auspicious time.

In India people say that between 4.00 am and 6.00 am is brahmamuhurta, which is why many Hindus and all yogis get up around 3 am, evacuate their bowels, clean their mouth, throat, pharynx, nasal tract, tongue and then do some asanas, pranayama and meditation. These people develop a wonderful temperament and their daily life is lived with vitality and awareness. They are not bothered by ill health, tiredness or weakness.

Previously it was mentioned that at the time of brahmamuhurta the pineal gland is active. Having swelled to its maximum size, the secretions of melatonin are taken into the blood and absorbed by the gonads, which in turn inhibits the sexual function, allowing the aspirant to keep his mind in the subtle planes of consciousness. This is a time of tranquillity and perfect relaxation of mental and physical tensions when great benefits can be gained. During brahmamuhurta the pituitary gland has its daily cycle of ACTH secretion, ACTH being one of the hormones of the pituitary gland. This hormone passes through the blood and stimulates the adrenal gland which, in turn, secretes sufficient adrenaline to the body so that it becomes filled with vital energy for the day's work. People who sleep through these precious hours merely burn up the valuable secretions and eliminate the energy through the physical body.

Arising early and practising yoga or just being awake and singing devotional songs is sufficient to charge the mind to the point where the excess energies, otherwise wasted through the physical system, are sublimated. These excess energies are evident as physical tension, very strong sexual desires, overheating of the body and frequent fever. It also manifests in the personality in the form of greed, compulsive eating, restlessness and sleeplessness.

The East has been aware for thousands of years of the spiritual and psychic importance of brahmamuhurta, and now the West has completed the picture with the discovery of the physical importance of the time from 3.30 am to 6.00 am. Let the people of the world arise at this magical hour, take a bath or shake off their tiredness, then go for a brisk walk, being constantly aware of their own movements, their breath and the passing scenery, sounds and smells. Everyone wanting a clear mind should get up at brahmamuhurta.

9

Yoga Practices for Awakening Ajna Chakra

Among the thousands of meditation techniques in yoga there are many practices for awakening this important ajna chakra. In all these meditation techniques it is required that one moves the awareness from the outer objective environment to the inner. The inner awareness is not different to the outer; the mind and senses have merely been withdrawn or partially withdrawn from the external environment. This inner awareness is always there, but the mind does not notice inner events when it is functioning with the outer objects. The complete withdrawal of the mind and the senses from the outer objects is called *pratyahara*.

By simply attempting to control the mind it is very difficult to withdraw it from the senses, but by using some inner form, sound or symbol, the mind will gradually turn inward and outer awareness will diminish. When the state of pratyahara is complete, when outer awareness has diminished to a point and then disappeared, the practitioner will not function on the external plane at all. He can be tapped with a stick, his name can be called, a sweet can be placed on his tongue, incense can be burnt, but he will not know about any of these events. This is an advanced stage of pratyahara and beginners will not be able to completely withdraw their awareness; however, this does not prevent them from proceeding with the meditation practices.

In fact, it is only by doing daily practice with strict regularity that the mind is trained so that, as the months pass by, the inner awareness gradually increases as the outer awareness diminishes. A beginner is advised to select his practices and perform them over a length of time that can be easily repeated day after day. Many beginners start out adventurously by sitting for one hour every morning, but soon the mind becomes tired and the joy of practising yoga turns into a burden and many days are missed. It is far better to do just a fifteen minute sitting every morning and night, with meticulous regularity, than a one hour sitting four days a week.

It is written in the upanishads that the state of mind while practising mediation is like boiling hot water; when the fire is withdrawn for a short time, it takes much longer to boil the water again after replacing the fire. Many gurus who know about the path of meditation say that to miss one practice in the daily routine is to revert right back to the beginning. In this way, months and years of effort can be lost in one day.

Actually, progress in the practices is not at all regular. Some days the mind goes very deep and some days it is so distracted by thoughts and feelings that the aspirant feels like stopping the practice because he thinks he is not suited. This is a misconception, for success comes to all who persist, but they must cling to their resolve to regularly do the practices with tenacity and zeal. The mind is like all other things in man, every day a little different.

The path of meditation practice is like the mountain path; the peaks are dazzling and illuminating, yet the depressions are fogged up with the vacillations and vicissitudes of the mind. On some days the mind is your friend and on other days it will lead you astray. It will tell you tales that will sound so convincing that definitely you will think it right, proper and just to give up the practices. If you are observant, you will not have to deny the mind; just watch it like a silent witness, silent in the knowledge that you will continue your practices. However, if you are not aware of the nature of the mind, you will have to proceed by the strength of resolve to daily continue the practice.

Note: To learn these yogic techniques correctly and in order to actually feel the individual effect of each instruction, it is recommended that the practices be learnt from an experienced teacher.

1. Jala Neti (nasal cleansing with water)

The first practice is a physical one, although its effects are psychic. This is jala neti, a process of passing water from the left nostril to the right and vice versa, using a small pot fitted with a stem which functions like a teapot. The end of the stem is cone shaped for a snug fit in the nostril. The water should be slightly salty and warm. Hold the head on the side with the neck bent slightly forward and, with the pot in the left hand, slowly pass water into the left nostril and let it run up to the sinuses and down the right nostril. After about ¼ litre of water has passed, repeat on the opposite side by passing water into the right nostril and out the left. While the water is passing, one has to be careful to keep the mouth open and to breathe through the mouth, taking special care not to breathe through the nose. Afterwards, the nostrils should be dried by rapid inhalation and exhalation through one nostril at a time, then both nostrils together, until the last drop of water has dried up.

Jala neti is primarily a hatha yoga practice, which massages the nerves around the *trikuti* (eyebrow centre) and stimulates the activity of this centre, facilitating the practices described later to awaken ajna. The nasal tracts are thoroughly cleaned, making it easy for the breath to pass freely through the nostrils.

Jala neti is easily done, but to ensure success it should be done at least once in the presence of a yoga teacher.

91

2. Asanas for Meditation

By practising the following postures, you will find which asana suits you best for meditation. The instructions and precautions in *Asana Pranayama Mudra Bandha* should be carefully observed.

Padmasana (lotus pose): *Padma* means lotus. During deep states of meditation the mind loses connection with the body and on such occasions padmasana (or siddhasana) holds the body steady, preventing it from falling. In deep meditation the hands should be placed on the knees.

The technique is performed from a sitting position. The right foot should be placed on the left thigh and the left foot on the right thigh. The hands may be placed on the knees in jnana or chin mudra.

Ardha padmasana (half lotus pose): *Ardha* means half; therefore this asana is the half lotus pose.

Place one foot under or against the opposite thigh and the other foot on top of the opposite thigh. Keep the back, neck and head straight.

Siddhasana (accomplished pose for men): *Siddha* means perfection; a siddha is a sage or a seer. This is a favourite pose of advanced yogis and adepts. It is probably the best asana for meditation because, when done correctly, it regulates the genito-urinary nerve flow and creates an excellent mood for meditation.

Place the right heel against the perineum and the sole against the left thigh. Bend the left leg and place the heel against the pubic bone. The ankles are situated one above the other. Insert the toes of the left foot between the thigh and calf of the right leg. The toes of the right foot are pulled up between the thigh and calf of the left leg. Place the hands on the knees in chin or jnana mudra.

Siddha Yoni Asana (accomplished pose for women): Siddha yoni asana is the female form of siddhasana. Bend the right leg, placing the sole of the foot flat against the inner left thigh and the heel firmly against the groin. Bend the left leg and place the foot on top of the right thigh, pulling the right toes up into the space between the left calf and thigh. The left heel is above the right heel.

By performing siddhasana or siddha yoni asana, moola bandha and vajroli mudra take place automatically, for in these poses the two heels cut off the genital nerve flow and direct the sexual energy impulses upward.

Sukhasana (easy pose): *Sukha* means easy; it is the easiest and most comfortable posture for japa and meditation.

Place the right foot under the left thigh, and the left foot under the right thigh. The hands are placed on the knees and the head, neck and back are straight but relaxed. Those who are extremely stiff may practise this asana by tying a cloth around the lower back and the knees.

3. Omkara or Om Chanting

This practice prepares the mind for the more advanced and powerful practices. *Omkara* is the name for the mantra *Om*. *Om* is the universal cosmic sound often described as the sacred trinity: creation, preservation and destruction in its three syllables. It is the sound made by opening the mouth wide and making the centre of sound vibration begin at the back of the throat and then progressing forward and simultaneously closing the mouth until the centre reaches the closed lips at the front with the sound *'mmm'*. It is said to represent the fullness or completeness of universal consciousness, because this chanting from the back of the mouth to the lips encompasses the full gamut of all possible sound. *Om* is the most powerful mantra and is suitable for all people. It renders the mind peaceful and tranquil.

Sit in a meditation asana and draw in the breath until the lungs are comfortably full. Chant *Om* softly with full awareness of the sound and imagine that it is emanating from the eyebrow centre. The chanting of each *Om* should be long, steady and of even pitch. This practice can be continued for up to two hours morning and night. One can begin with five minutes and gradually work up to longer times so that the daily practice becomes powerful and effective in awakening ajna.

The next technique not only makes the mind tranquil, but also increases the power of the mind's concentration on the point of ajna. Chant *Om* rapidly so that each lasts for no longer than 1½ seconds; in one minute 40 *Om* mantras may be chanted. The mantra should be directed towards the eyebrow centre as if a spear were being directed towards this point, repeated with regularity and an even beat with the precise timing of a clock. The mantras should be so continuous that each mantra runs into the next, being careful not to change the sound to *'mo'*. This practice is even more powerful when done by a group of enthusiasts. Then the chanting should be in unison.

An alternate site for directing the force of the mantra is the lower point of ajna at the top of the spine, near the inferior brain. This point can be found by following the technique for discovering ajna chakra through contraction of mooladhara, described in *Kundalini Tantra*.

4. Japa

Japa is a practice followed by many religions. In the science of yoga, the guru gives the mantra to the disciple, knowing the science of mantra and its effect on the mind. The function of the mantra is to penetrate the deeper layers of the mind. The different vibrations each mantra gives by its repetition affect centres in the brain and thus bring about an awakening of these centres.

The immediate benefit of the mantra is to bring peace to the mind by positively modifying the condition of the brain through release of mental tensions. This having been effected, the mind is sated and will not be an obstacle to further and deeper awakening. The ultimate aim is to bring about a psychic and spiritual awakening.

This tantric system of awakening is so powerful that premature progress can cause much damage, for when ajna is awakened the mind is open to great amounts of energy so that thoughts become very powerful. To the untrained mind a small troubling thought which cannot be controlled will develop into such vast dimensions that a mental holocaust can result. Until the guru initiates the disciple with a special mantra, *Om* should be used because it is universal and suits every temperament.

A mala of 108 beads is used with mantra repetition. Hold the mala between the third and fourth fingers and the thumb of the right hand and rotate the beads one by one with the rhythm of the mantra. The *sumeru* (terminal bead) should never be crossed; when it is reached, turn the mala and reverse the direction of rotation. The mala can be made from tulsi (holy basil) wood, crystal, lotus seed or rudraksha nuts. The mantra is powerful and, when used in conjunction with a mala, the mala becomes charged with its vibration. For this reason it is best to keep the mala in a silk bag when out of use and not to let other people use it because of their different vibrations.

The first technique, called *baikhari*, is to repeat the mantra aloud. After some time, the second technique may be introduced, called *upanshu*, where the mantra is whispered so that only the practitioner can hear it. The third technique, called *manasic*, is to repeat the mantra mentally without movement of the lips. Manasic japa is more powerful than baikhari or upanshu. The most powerful process of repetition just goes on by itself without the conscious willing of the practitioner; this is called *ajapa japa*.

First baikhari japa should be practised by repeating the mantra aloud continuously. When the breath is exhausted, continue mentally together with the rotation of the mala as the breath is being inhaled. Each mantra should move with its own force and vibration towards *bhrumadhya*, the eyebrow centre, or to the contact point at the top of the spine. Gradually progress to the same technique with upanshu and finally with manasic japa.

The practice of japa with awareness on ajna has a purifying effect on the chakra. This practice is called *chakra shodhanam*, a tantric practice in which a certain number of malas are practised on each chakra in turn. The experiences during this practice at ajna can be quite enthralling because of the psychic nature of this chakra. Many psychic adventures can be experienced; for example, the whole body (actually the psychic body) can appear to hover over the asana, the weight of the body seemingly reduced to nothing. Often lights appear, or the characteristic white light of ajna. An eye may be seen, maybe your own eye looking at you from the eyebrow centre. The vibrations of the mantra pulse through the chakra and then all over the body up and down the spine and throughout the brain.

Needless to say, ajna shodhanam is a very important practice in the awakening of this chakra. It is the precursor to success with the tantric techniques using specialized mantras, yantras and mandalas.

5. Kaya Sthairyam

Kaya sthairyam means body steadiness and is the first stage in all meditation practices. In order to create a basis for concentration in which the faculties of the mind can be withdrawn from the body, it must be under perfect control. It is very difficult for even an advanced yogi to control the mind, but it is possible, even for a beginner, to control the body; and through control over the steadiness of the physical body and awareness of it, the mind automatically becomes relaxed.

Sit in a meditation asana, with the eyes closed, spine straight, the head erect and the hands on the knees in chin mudra. Systematically relax the body, starting with the right foot, ankle, calf muscle, thigh, hip, left foot, ankle, calf muscle and so on through every part of the body. Extend the awareness to the whole of the body so that it can be felt or seen with the mind, be aware of every part of the body as one object. Simultaneously mentally repeat, "the whole body, the whole body" until the whole body is felt as one. This stage will take about two or three minutes.

Then focus on body steadiness. First check the position, ensuring that the spine is absolutely straight, the head is erect and the body is relaxed. Mentally repeat, "for the next five minutes, I will be steady, I will be still, I will not move a muscle or limb." Do not allow any unconscious movements of the fingers or toes and, no matter how strong the urge to move or adjust the position, relieve a small pain or scratch an itch, do not move. Often with beginners, the body starts to twitch, vibrate, or shake. If this happens, apply willpower and keep saying, "I will be steady, I will be still." Sit like a statue, absolutely calm, absolutely quiet, absolutely still like a rock. This is the idea to imprint on the mind in order to be successful.

Having gained initial control over the body, continue the practice until a change comes. The body will appear to change so that all the body seems to be within the mind. The weight of the body apparently decreases and it may feel as if the body is not sitting heavily on the floor as before, but floating a few inches above it. The body begins to get a stiffness and stillness so that even if there is a desire to move, the reaction is not coordinated. This is called psychic stiffening of the body, and the stage of stiffening is necessary for more advanced practices.

By doing this practice for half an hour, daily progress will be very fast. In the beginning start in a very disciplined manner for about five minutes and gradually increase the length of sitting. Kaya sthairyam is a sadhana in itself and if practised for three or so hours, with perfect control over the body, will culminate in samadhi, the goal of yoga. However, in this context we are interested in the quick achievement of psychic stiffening, which is the basis for the next lesson.

6. Trataka

Trataka is the first of the practices in the series that require and develop concentration. The power of the mind is great but dissipated through so many desires and energy wasting pastimes. By consolidating the widely spread mental shakti and applying it to one purpose, be it spiritual or worldly, power is restored.

In order to concentrate on an object, either internal or external, the mind must either be under control so that distractions are kept away, or the mind should enjoy or get some feeling of bliss or comfort by concentrating on this object. To do this the object has to be selected on an individual basis. Some people can get bliss and good concentration by becoming aware of the picture of their guru, the form of the mantra *Om*, a flower, the rising sun, the moon in an open sky or the flame of a candle. Of all these, the candle flame is the most convenient and practical object to take up for beginners.

Trataka on an outer object is the best practice of concentration in the beginning because it is easier for the untrained mind. The mind has the habit of attaching itself to outside objects, whereas when we close our eyes to concentrate on an inner symbol or point the mind constantly wavers. The mind, when operating through the medium of the senses, actually loses energy and when concentrating on an inner object, withdrawn from the senses, gains energy. This process of gaining energy always requires some sort of effort of will. However, on the outer object, the mind can happily dwell on the object, for it is as natural for the mind to do this as it is for rivers to flow from the mountains to the sea. The candle flame is an ideal object to begin with because of its fine shape and colour. There is a natural attraction for the flame, and all enjoy its beauty, radiance and aura.

The place to practise trataka is in a dark room. The doors and windows should be closed and the curtains drawn so that the room is completely dark except for the solitary light of the candle. There should be no wind or draught, so that the candle flame will be perfectly steady. Sit in a meditation asana and place the candle directly in front of the nose so the flame is not higher than the eyebrow centre or lower than the chin. The candle should be about two feet from the eyes or at a distance at which the eyes can focus on the candle comfortably without strain. The distance will vary according to the individual.

Closing the eyes, practise kaya sthairyam until the whole body has reached the point of psychic stiffening, then open the eyes and focus on the candle flame. Concentrate on one point in the flame, just above the wick, where the colour changes, at the one point where the tinge of colour of the flame is different, maybe red or blue or bright yellow. Gaze at the point with full attention, ideally without blinking, for about three minutes without straining. The body must not move, nor should the eyes.

Close the eyes and be aware of the inner image remaining; it is a small seed-shaped light, maybe yellow, green or red. Maybe, in the first practices, if there is tension, the seed of light will not appear; however, with persistence it will come into the inner view. Maintain constant steadiness of the body and constant awareness of the seed. After a short time the image may move up into chidakasha, in the region of the forehead, or in some other direction. However it moves, follow the movement until it disappears out of sight. Continue internal image awareness until it ceases to reappear, at which time open the eyes and repeat the practice. Between each round of trataka adjust the position if needed, but stillness and steadiness of the body must be re-established.

This practice of outer trataka is excellent for preparing for inner trataka and meditation on ajna. The eyesight is strengthened, the mind is calmed and the faculty of visualization is aided. Trataka brings the practitioner to a point in sadhana where control of the psychic realm is required, which hitherto has just been an experience.

In the next stage of trataka the internal image is observed very carefully, and as soon as it starts to move it is brought back to the eyebrow centre. This advanced technique requires willpower; for it is only by willing that the image can be held steady. In the final stage of outer trataka, visualize the whole candle when the eyes are closed; the flame, the wick, the candle and the stand on which the candle rests. Do not just imagine it, but actually try to see or visualize, the whole image internally.

To be able to achieve clear visualization of an outer object indicates an advanced ability in concentration and this practice should be repeated without tension until success

99

is achieved. This outer trataka is called in Sanskrit *bahiranga trataka* and is a necessary precursor of the next practice, *antar trataka*, or inner trataka.

7. Antar Trataka

This is the first fully psychic practice, where one becomes aware of not an outer object but an inner object or point. This practice requires peace of mind and steadiness of the body.

First practise kaya sthairyam up to the point of psychic stiffening, then become aware of the breath in the throat; just be constantly aware of the psychic breath flowing in and out. This psychic breathing is a powerful tool for pacifying the mind. Each breath should be perfectly natural, sometimes a little longer and sometimes a little shorter, but simply observe or feel it going in and out. On inhalation the psychic breath moves up the trunk, and on exhalation it moves down. As tensions are relaxed the breath speed will slow down until it is hardly moving, and all that is felt is the subtle breath drifting through the throat area.

When the breath has been followed for about fifteen minutes, move the awareness to the eyebrow centre and become aware of a tiny star. Visualize the star and keep it in constant view. Maybe, in the beginning, it will only flash for an instant, but that is enough for the beginning and from there the faculty of visualization will develop.

8. Shambhavi Mudra

Shambhavi is sometimes called *bhrumadhya drishti*. Shambhavi was a princess who practised this mudra for Shiva, her beloved lord, and joined with him. By the practice of shambhavi mudra we can also join with Shiva. In the trinity Shiva is the destroyer of created things and also the destroyer of obstacles that prevent man from progressing mentally, morally and spiritually.

Sit in a meditation asana with the spine and head erect. First look at one point directly in front, then, without moving the head and by rolling the eyes up, look up as high as possible and concentrate, with eyes open, on the point between the eyebrows. As an aid the thumb can be held in front of the nose with the arm stretched out; the eyes are focused on the thumb, which should be raised until the eyes cannot follow its movement any further. It is at this point that the eyes are focused on the eyebrow centre. This practice can be continued for as long as possible or until strain is felt in the muscles of the eyes. Then the eyes are closed and relaxed, and after a short time, keeping the body still, shambhavi mudra is repeated up to ten times.

Shambhavi mudra is beneficial in directing the mind to bhrumadhya, and it awakens the mind's natural ability to concentrate while directing the mental, psychic and pranic forces to this point. Shambhavi mudra is a necessary precursor of later practices designed to awaken ajna and should be combined with khechari mudra for enhanced effectiveness.

9. Khechari Mudra

This practice is given because it enhances the effectiveness of shambhavi mudra. *Khe* means 'sky' and *charya* means 'one who moves'. The name of this practice is such because it produces a state of mind in which the astral body, the body of feelings, becomes detached from the physical body. The consciousness dwells in *akasha,* the space between the astral and physical worlds. This practice should only be attempted in close relationship with a guru.

Sitting in a meditation asana, roll the tongue back against the upper palate whilst keeping the teeth closed. In full khechari mudra the tongue is rolled back and up into the space between the eyebrows, but for this simple practice it is sufficient that the tongue is rolled back so that the tip is embedded into the soft palate behind the bony structure in the roof of the mouth. When the tongue reaches the upper passage of the nose, sweet liquid produced by the salivary glands is tasted.

One who masters this technique is able to practise *kumbhaka* (breath retention) for as long as he wishes. Yogis who have had themselves buried alive for days and even weeks utilize khechari mudra to sustain themselves. This mudra activates the nectar glands, which are related to ajna. Khechari mudra awakens kundalini shakti and preserves vital energies. In khechari mudra the jaw muscles may become tired after some time. When this point is reached, the tongue should be relaxed, the excess saliva swallowed, and after a short time khechari reapplied.

These practices should be combined by first performing khechari mudra, followed by shambhavi mudra, then releasing shambhavi mudra before khechari mudra.

10. Anuloma Viloma

The meaning of this Sanskrit term is up-down. In this practice the up and down movement of the breath is followed by the awareness. Practise kaya sthairyam until psychic stiffening is reached and then become aware of the breath in the nostrils. Feel the breath moving in and out of the left nostril, then the right nostril and then be aware of the breath as it flows in and out of both nostrils together.

In this practice the flow of the breath in each nostril is mentally controlled by consciously inhaling through the left, exhaling through the right, inhaling through the right and exhaling through the left. This is one round. In this way practise four rounds and then breathe in and out of both nostrils simultaneously. This is the fifth round. Continue in this manner while counting rounds from 100 to zero. Maintain accuracy in the counting and, if an error is made, begin again.

For the awakening of ajna there is one important additional point in the technique. On inhalation the whole consciousness should move with the breath from the end of the nose up to the eyebrow centre, and on exhalation the whole consciousness should flow out from the eyebrow centre to the end of the nose together with the breath.

It is very important to keep count of the breath because anuloma viloma is so powerful that, without counting, awareness may be swallowed up by the unconscious sphere, and it is the aim of this practice to stimulate ajna on the psychic or subconscious level only. In the unconscious sphere there is awareness only of the vast store of impressions in the unconscious mind and not of the practice. Awareness of the practice is essential for the development of mind control and concentration on ajna.

11. Maha Mudra

Maha mudra is a technique described in detail in the tantric texts. When it is practised, the energy of the breath is directed towards the eyebrow centre. Sit in siddhasana / siddha yoni asana or padmasana with the hands resting on the knees. Breathe in and imagine or feel the breath filling the stomach and chest from the navel upwards. When capacity has been reached, perform jalandhara and moola bandha.

Jalandhara bandha is performed by pushing up the shoulders with straightened arms and bending the head forward until the chin touches the chest. Moola bandha acts on mooladhara, located in the perineum in males and the cervix in females, and is performed by contracting this area, though actually it is a psychic contraction. To initiate this psychic contraction, however, the physical contraction must be performed.

Once the bandhas have been performed, move the awareness to trikuti (eyebrow centre) and feel the psychic pressure created at this point. Continue for as long as the breath can be held comfortably. Mentally repeat, "Trikuti, trikuti, trikuti," until retention cannot be maintained. At this time, release jalandhara bandha before exhaling, feeling as if the breath was going down to the navel. People who suffer from heart disease or epilepsy should not do this practice.

12. Trikuti Nadi Shodhanam

In trikuti there is a pulsating nadi on the rhythm of which *Om* is felt pulsating. Practise kaya sthairyam until psychic stiffness is achieved, then move the consciousness to trikuti, and there try to feel the pulsating nadi. If you do not have success, you will have to persist until you find the beating nadi. If it cannot be found, then move the consciousness back a little in a straight line to a point approximately between the ears and search for it again. If still there is no success, then use the imagination and mentally start the pulsating of the nadi. It is like the steady simple beating of a small drum in trikuti.

When fully established with the beating pulse, feel the mantra *Om* with the rhythm of the pulsating nadi and continue the awareness of pulsation and mantra for at least 15 minutes. Then, without moving or changing the asana, proceed on to the next practice directly.

13. Guru Chakra Bheda

In guru chakra bheda the force of the mantra is coupled with the force of the psychic breath, so that the mantra pierces its way into the chakra. Continuing from the previous practice of trikuti nadi shodhanam, with inhalation the awareness travels from trikuti to the rear centre of ajna at the top of the spine. With exhalation, the awareness returns to trikuti. The breath for this practice should be short and gentle.

Once established in the movement of the psychic breath, backward to the spinal top and forward to the eyebrow centre, add the mantra *Om* with the rhythm of the breath, so that the outgoing forward moving breath together with the mantra breaks into the trikuti centre.

This practice involves a psychic breathing passage, this being different to the path of the gross breath. The gross breath moves through the physical respiratory system and the psychic breath moves in harmony with the gross breath, there being many paths for the psychic breath in the body. In the beginning the psychic breath is moved with imagination, but as experience is gained, its natural flow is discovered. In other words, in the beginning, the psychic breath is just imagination, but after some practice it becomes a real experience.

The *Om* mantra should be felt going backwards and forwards and an attempt should be made to deepen the experience, even though this will come about by itself.

14. Ajapa Japa

Ajapa japa is a practice that must be taught by a teacher or guru in order to obtain good results. This subject has been discussed by Swami Satyananda Saraswati in the books *Mechanics of Meditation*, *Dynamics of Yoga* and *Meditation from the Tantras*, and has been exhaustively treated by Swami Niranjanananda Saraswati in *Dharana Darshan*.

The tongue is placed in khechari mudra and ujjayi pranayama is performed, so that the mantra *So Ham* is in harmony with the natural breath: *So* for the ingoing breath and *Ham* for the outgoing breath. The psychic path of the breath is in the spinal column between mooladhara and ajna. *So*, the inhaled breath, moves from mooladhara to ajna and *Ham*, the exhaled breath, moves from ajna to mooladhara.

15. Meditation on Trikuti

This is the last and most powerful practice for awakening ajna. Though this method is simple the mind must be prepared for meditation.

The first step is to sit in kaya sthairyam until stiffness is attained. Then move the awareness to *trikuti*, the eyebrow centre, and hold it there with constant awareness, without wavering. From this point one can transcend the body and dive deep into ajna, deep into the psychic lands of multi-coloured, multi-variable vibrational experiences.

Appendix

Sat Chakra Nirupanam

Sat Chakra Nirupanam (description of six chakras) is a text on kundalini yoga. This Appendix contains the transliteration of verses 32–38 on ajna chakra as well as a detailed translation and commentary by Arthur Avalon (in *The Serpent Power*, 1919) on the original text by Acharya Swami Poornananda, Bengal (circa 1500 AD) in 1919. *Sat Chakra Nirupanam* is not an exhaustive treatise on kundalini and we have to reach for other texts to reveal the whole gamut of recorded experiences in kundalini yoga. S.S. Goswami in his book *Laya Yoga* (1980) has studied and analyzed hundreds of texts, including manuscripts from private collections, and has added many details and created a reference for the avid student.

Verse 32

Aajnaanaamaambujam taddhimakarasadrisham dhyaanadhaama-
prakaasham; hakshaabhyaam vai kalaabhyaam parilasitava-
purnetrapatram sushubhram. Tanmadhye haakinee saa
shashisamadhavalaa vaktrashatkam dadhaanaa; vidyaam mudraam
kapaalam damarujapavateem bibhratee shuddhachittaa.

Translation

The lotus named ajna is like the moon (beautifully white).
On its two petals are the letters Ha and Ksha, which are also
white and enhance its beauty. It shines with the glory of
dhyana (the state of mind acquired by meditation). Inside is
Shakti Hakini, whose six faces are like so many moons. She
has six arms, in one of which she holds a book; two others
are lifted up in the gestures of dispelling fear and granting
boons, and with the rest she holds a skull, a small drum
(damaru), and a rosary. Her mind is pure *(shuddha chitta)*.

Commentary (Avalon)

The author describes ajna chakra between the eyebrows in
the seven verses beginning with this:

'The lotus named ajna' *(ajna nama)*: "Ajna of the guru is
communicated here, hence it is called ajna." Here between
the eyebrows is the ajna (command), which is communicated.
from above, hence it is called ajna. This lotus which is well
known is here. It is here that ajna of the guru is communicated

This lotus is between the eyebrows, as the following shows.
"Going upwards after entering the throat and palate, the
white and auspicious lotus between the eyebrows is reached
by kundali. It has two petals on which are the letters Ha and
Ksha, and it is the place of mind *(manas)*."

The following are descriptions of the lotus:

'Like the moon, beautifully white *(hima-kara-sadrisham)*.'
This comparison with chandra *(hima-kara)* may also mean
that this lotus is cool like moonbeams (the moon being the
receptacle of *amrita*, or nectar, whose characteristic is
coolness), and that it is also beautifully white.

It has been said in *Ishvara-Kartikeya-Samvada*: "Ajna chakra is above it; it is white and has two petals; the letters Ha and Ksha, variegated in colour, also enhance its beauty. It is the seat of mind *(manas)*."

'Two petals' *(netra-patra)*: the petals of the lotus.

'The letters Ha and Ksha, which are also white' *(ha-kshabhyam kalaa-bhyam parilasitavapuh su-shubhram)*: These two letters are by their very nature white, and by their being on the white petals the whiteness thereof is made more charming by this very excess of whiteness. (Or the meaning may be that the ajna chakra has rays cool like the ambrosial rays of the moon and like the moon beautifully white.) The letters are called kalaas because they are bijas of kalaas.

'It shines with the glory of dhyana' *(dhyana-dhama-prakasham)*: That is, its body shines like the glory of dhyana shakti.

'Hakini': He next speaks of the presence of Shakti Hakini. The force of the pronoun saa (she) in addition to her name is that she is the well-known Hakini.

'The gestures of dispelling fear and granting boons' *(mudra)*: There should be six weapons in her hands as she has six hands. There are some who read vidya and mudra as one word, *vidya-mudra,* and interpret it to mean *vyakhya-mudra* – the gesture that conveys learning or knowledge – and speak of her as possessed of four arms. Different manuscripts give different readings. The wise reader should judge for himself.

In a dhyana in another place she is thus described: "Meditate upon Her, the divine Hakini. She abides in the marrow and is white. In her hands are the damaru, the rudraksha rosary, the skull, the vidya (the sign of the book), the mudra (gesture of granting boons and dispelling fear). She has six red-coloured faces with three eyes in each. She is fond of food cooked with turmini, and is elated by drinking ambrosia. She is well seated on a white lotus, and her mind is exalted by the drink of the king of the devas gathered from the ocean."

110

Other commentary

S.S. Goswami makes reference to Kalicharana's interpretation of *Sat Chakra Nirupana*. Here 'like the moon' means 'moon-like white colour', adding that it may also mean that as the moon has nectarous cool rays, so ajna chakra is cool rayed. Also the commentator Ramawallabha says it is like the colour of the moon, and Vishwanatha explains that it causes moisture (from nectar) like the moon. In *Rudrayamala* we learn that in the hollow of ajna chakra is an excellent fluid, indicating there is nectar in ajna as there is in the moon.

Supporting the fact that ajna has two petals, Goswami cites some 25 texts, including manuscripts, upanishads and tantras. He also gives references to support descriptions that the petals are white and further references to the petals having lightning-like colour. Also, as has been mentioned in chapter 6, Swami Satyananda has described it as an 'intangible colour', meaning it cannot be easily defined, formulated or grasped.

So we have various descriptions of the same experience. As Shankaracharya said, "There is only one truth and the wise describe it in different ways."

In *Kalika Purana* (55.30), as reported by S.S. Goswami, at the point of confluence of the three nadis, ida, pingala and sushumna, is a six-cornered red hexagon magnified to four fingers breadth, and this is what is called ajna chakra by the yogis. *Rudrayamala* part 2 (20:6–7) states that within ajna is the beautiful *kama chakra* (desire chakra) and inside this is the very subtle prashna chakra and inside that the phala chakra. Goswami suggests these are for very special concentration.

About Hakini, Goswami cites the following references. In *Kalicharana*, Hakini is white with six red faces, each with three eyes, and six items in her hands. In *Kankalamalini Tantra*, Hakini's colour is a mixture of white, black and red; she is two-armed; her face is moonlike with beautiful rolling eyes like a moving black bee; she shines with the vermillion mark on her forehead; she has curled hair and is clad in red raiment and her upper garment is white.

111

In *Kularnava Tantra*, Hakini is dark blue and has one, two, three, four, five and six faces (according to the type of concentration) which glitter like the stars. She holds a skull spear, shield and abhaya mudra: One face indicates concentration in which 'I-ness' has been dissolved; two faces indicate concentration in which I-ness remains; three faces represent the three primary attributes; four faces represent gross sensory knowledge, super sensory knowledge, pre-sensory knowledge and non-sensory knowledge; five faces represent knowledge of the attributes of the five chakras below; six faces represent perceptual knowledge, thoughts and attention.

In *Kaulavalitantra*, she is white, has three eyes, holds a rudraksha mala, drum, skull, book, bow and the mudra of dispelling fear or granting boons.

Goswami concludes that concentration on Hakini gives the practitioner all the powers to continue work in ajna chakra. The six faces representing the five principles of the lower chakras plus manas. The third eye is concentration-light and the other eyes indicate perceptual knowledge, thoughts, attention and concentration-knowledge of three forms: dharana, dhyana and samadhi. If her faces are red in colour, it indicates kundalini knowledge and the white colour indicates a highly rarefied form of sattwa. Dark blue indicates sattwa ready to proceed to a formless state, red colour indicates fully aroused kundalini in form and a mixture of white, red and black indicates harmonious balance of the three attributes.

Verse 33

Etatpadmaantaraale nivasati cha manah sookshmaroopam prasiddham; yonau tatkarnikaayaamitarashivapadam lingachihna-prakaasham. Vidyunmaalaavilaasam paramakulapadam brahma-sootraprabodham; vedaanaamaadibeejam sthiratarahridayash-chintayettatkramena.

Translation

Within this lotus dwells the subtle mind (manas). It is well-known. Inside the yoni in the pericarp is the Shiva called Itara in His phallic form. He here shines like a chain of lightning flashes. The first bija of the vedas (Om), which is the abode of the most excellent Shakti and which by its lustre makes visible the Brahmasutra, is also there. The sadhaka with steady mind should meditate upon these according to the order (prescribed).

Commentary (Avalon)

He speaks of the presence of manas in this lotus.

'Subtle' *(sukshma roopa)*: Manas is beyond the scope of the senses; that being so, it may be asked, what is the proof of its existence? The answer is it is well-known or universally accepted *(prasiddha)* and handed down from *anadi-purusha*, generation after generation as a thing realized, and is hence well-known. The evidence of the shastras, also, is that this manas selects and rejects. Here is the place of manas. The presence of manas is above the first bija of the vedas as will appear from what is about to be spoken of.

'Phallic form' *(linga-chihna-prakasham)*: He next speaks of the presence of the Shivalinga in the yoni which is within the pericarp. The Itara-Shiva who is there is in his phallic form, and within the yoni. Within the triangle in the pericarp dwells Itara-Shivapada, i.e. the Shiva known by the name of Itara. This linga is in the phallic form and white. As has been said in the *Bhuta-Shuddhi-Tantra*: "Inside it is the linga Itara, crystalline and with three eyes." Linga resembles continuous streaks of lightning flashes *(vidyun-mala-vilasam)*.

'First bija of the vedas' *(vedanam-adibeejam)*: He then speaks of the presence of the Pranava (Om) in the pericarp of this lotus. In the pericarp there is also the first bija, i.e. Pranava (ॐ).

'Which is the abode of the most excellent Shakti' *(parama-kulapada)*: *Kula* = Shakti, which is here of a triangular form. *Parama* means most excellent, by reason of its resembling lightning and like luminous substances; and *pada* means place, i.e. the triangular space. Hence this bija, namely the Pranava, we perceive is within the triangle. This is clearly stated as follows:

"Within the pericarp and placed in the triangle is Atma in the form of the Pranava, and above it, like the flame of a lamp, is the charming nada and bindu, which is makara, and above it is the abode of manas."

Now, if the parama-kulapada is the container (*adhara*) of and therefore inseparate from the Pranava, how is it that it is separately mentioned as one of the sixteen adharas spoken of in the following passage? For it has been said that "the sixteen adharas hard of attainment by the yogi are mooladhara, swadhisthana, manipura, anahata, vishuddha, ajna, bindu, kalapada, nibhodhika, arddhendu, nada, nadanta, unmani, vishnu-vaktra, dhruvamandala and Shiva."

The answer is that the second kulapada is not the one in ajna chakra; it is in the vacant space above mahanada which is spoken of later. This will become clear when dealing with the subject of mahanada.

'Which makes manifest the Brahma-sutra' (*brahma-sutra-prabodha*): Brahma-sutra = chitrini-nadi. This nadi is made visible by the lustre of the Pranava. In verse 3 this nadi has been described as 'lustrous with the lustre of the Pranava'.

The sadhaka should with a steady mind meditate upon all these, viz., Hakini, Manas, Itara linga and Pranava in the order prescribed. This is different from the order in which they are placed in the text by the author. But the arrangement of words according to their import is to be preferred to their positions in the text. The order as shown here should prevail. Thus, first Hakini in the pericarp; in the triangle above her Itara-linga; in the triangle above him the Pranava; and last of all, above the Pranava itself, manas should be meditated upon.

Other commentary

In verse 33 of *Laya Yoga*, Goswami says that subtle manas has a centre of operation beyond the ordinary senses and *antarala*

114

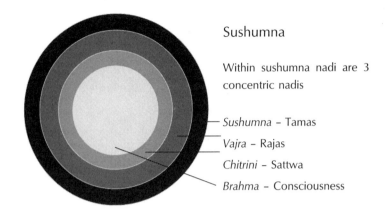

Sushumna

Within sushumna nadi are 3 concentric nadis

Sushumna – Tamas
Vajra – Rajas
Chitrini – Sattwa
Brahma – Consciousness

(within) indicates there is a sub-centre within ajna where manas is.

Goswami further refers to the order as per Kalicharana's commentary on *Sat Chakra Nirupana*, saying not to take the order given, but the order of importance, i.e. 1. Hakini, 2. Itaralingam, 3. Pranava and 4. Manas.

Brahma sutra is Brahma nadi according to Shankara, Vishwanatha, Bhuwanamohana and Ramavallabha, but Kalicharana says that it means chitrini nadi, which is concurred with by Avalon.

Antarala (first word of the verse): According to Goswami the use of this word explains that within ajna is a subsystem of chakras leading up to sahasrara.

Goswami's translation is: It is well known that the seat of the subtle manas is at an intermediate point of this lotus; inside the pericarp of this is a triangle *(yoni)*, which is the seat of *Itarashiva* (Shiva endowed with the power of full control over desires) who is revealed in his linga form (absorptive concentration form, *linga chihna prakasha*). Here is also the seat of the supreme power of kundalini *(paramakula)*. Like the streaks of lightning flashes causing the rousing of the Brahma nadi and manifesting as the first bija of the vedas, that is the first mantra (Om) on which a practitioner should do thought concentration according to the order (prescribed by the guru).

115

Verse 34

Dhyaanaatmaa saadhakendro bhavati parapure sheeghragaamee muneendrah; sarvajnah sarvadarshee sakalahitakarah sarvashaastraarthavetta. Advaitaachaaravaadee vilasati paramaapoorvasiddhiprashiddho; deerghaayuh so'pi kartaa tribhuvanabhavane samhritau paalane cha.

Translation

The excellent sadhaka, whose Atma is nothing but a meditation on this lotus, is able quickly to enter another's body at will, and becomes the most excellent among munis, and all-knowing and all-seeing. He becomes the benefactor of all, and versed in all the shastras. He realizes his unity with the Brahman and acquires excellent and unknown powers *(siddhis)*. Full of fame and long-lived, he ever becomes the creator, destroyer and preserver of the three worlds.

Commentary (Avalon)

In this verse he speaks of the good to be gained by the dhyana of this lotus.

'Most excellent among munis' *(munindra)*: A muni is one who is accomplished in dhyana and yoga and other excellent acquirements. The suffix 'indra' means king or chieftain and is added to names to signify excellence.

'Versed in all the shastras' *(sarva-shastrarthavetta)*: Such a one becomes proficient in the shastras and in divine knowledge and thus he becomes all-seeing *(sarva-darshi)*, i.e. able to look at things from all points by reason of his being possessed of wisdom and knowledge which harmonizes with shastras, manners and customs.

'He realizes . . .' *(advaitachara-vadi)*: He knows that this universe and all material existence is the Brahman, from such sayings of Shruti as, "The worlds are its pada (that is amshas)"; "All that exists is the Brahman"; and "I am the deva and no one else; I am the very Brahman, and sorrow is not my share." He knows that the Brahman alone is the Real *(Sat)* and everything else is unreal *(asat)*, and that they all shine by the light of the Brahman. The man who by such knowledge is able to realize the identity of the individual with the Supreme Spirit (*jivatman* and *paramatman*) and preaches it, is an Advaitavadi.

'Excellent and unknown powers' (*paramapoorva-siddhi*): that is, most exalted and excellent powers.

'Full of fame' (*prasiddha*): i.e. famous by reason of his excellence.

'He ever becomes . . .' (*so'pi karta tribhuvana-bhavane samhritau palane cha*): This is *prashamsha-vada*, i.e. praise, or it may mean that such a sadhaka becomes absorbed in the Supreme on the dissolution of the body, and thus becomes the source of creation, preservation and destruction.

Verse 35

Tadantashchakre'sminnivasati satatam shuddhabuddhyantaraatmaa;
pradeepaabhajyotihpranavavirachanaaroopavarnaprakaashah.
Tadoordhve chandraardhastadupari vilasadbinduroopee makaara-
stadoordhve naado'sau baladhavalasudhaadhaarasantaanahaasee.

Translation

Within the triangle in this chakra ever dwells the combination of letters (AUM, or Om, which form the Pranava or mantra ॐ). It is the inner Atma as pure mind (buddhi) and resembles a flame in its radiance. Above it is the crescent moon and above this again is ma-kara, shining in its form of bindu. Above this is nada, whose whiteness equals that of Balarama and diffuses the rays of the moon.

Commentary (Avalon)

The author desires to speak of the presence of the Pranava in ajna and says that in this chakra, and within the triangle which has already been spoken of, ever dwells the combination of the letters A and U, which by the rules of *sandhi* (union) make the thirteenth vowel O. This combination of letters is *shuddha-buddhyantaratma*, i.e. the innermost spirit manifesting as pure intelligence (*buddhi*).

117

The question may be asked if the thirteenth vowel (O) is that. To obviate this, the author (Poornananda) qualifies it by saying 'above it is the half moon etc.' It is by adding the half moon (nada) and bindu to O that the Pranava is formed.

He next gives its attributes: 'Resembles a flame in its radiance' *(pradipabha jyotih)*: But how can this thirteenth vowel by itself be shuddha-buddhyantaratma? He therefore says, "Above it is the crescent moon *(tadoordhve chandrardhah)*. And above this again is ma-kara, shining in its form of bindu *(tadupari vilasad-bindu-roopi makarah)*." It is thus shown that by the placing of the crescent moon and the bindu over the thirteenth vowel the Pranava is completely formed.

'Above this is nada' *(tadoordhve nado'sau)*, i.e. above the Pranava is the *avantara* (final or second) nada, which challenges as it were the whiteness of Baladeva and the moon *(bala-dhavala-sudha-dhara-santana hasee)*. By this he means to say that it is extremely white, excelling in whiteness both Baladeva and the rays of the moon.

Some read *tadadye nado'sau* (in the place of *tadoordhve nado'sau*) and interpret it as, "Below bindu-roopi ma-kara is nada", but that is incorrect. The text says, "Above this, again, is ma-kara, shining in its form of bindu," and there is nada below it; that being so, it is useless to repeat that nada is below.

Besides, this nada is beyond the nada, which forms part of the Pranava, and is part of the differentiating *(bhidyamana)* Para-bindu placed above the Pranava. If, however, it be urged that it is necessary to state the details in describing the special Pranava *(vishishta-pranava)*, and it is asked, "Why do you say a second nada is inappropriate?" then the reading *tadadye nado'sau* may be accepted.

But read thus it should be interpreted in the following manner: "This nada shown below the *bindu-roopi ma-kara* is *bala-dhavala-sudha-dhara-samthana-hasee,* and the nada first spoken of is also so described. Such repetition is free from blame on the authority of the maxim that "the great are subject to no limitations."

Commentary (general)

Balarama was born as the brother of Krishna. Balarama is a symbol of strength, an obedient son, an ideal brother and husband, an ideal man and god. He is a protector from desires, the divinity of strength of the divine, symbolizing duty, honesty and simplicity. Vishnu incarnated as Balarama when Indra and the other gods came to Lord Vishnu and asked for release from the demon son Kamsa, King of Mathura. Vishnu took one black and one white hair from his head and promised that these two would come to fight against the demons. This way, first Balarama (the white hair) then Krishna (the black hair) incarnated in the womb of Devaki.

Goswami states that about the Pranava it has been said that there is the bija in akshara form which is explained in *Soubhajnalakshmyupanishad* as a splendorous consciousness-like light on which concentration should be done.

Yogarajopanishad says that circular light indicates luminous coils of kundalini.

Verse 36

Iha sthaane leene susukhasadane chetasi puram niraalambaam badhvaa paramagurusevaasuviditaam.Tadabhyaasaad yogee pavanasuhridaam pashyati kanaan tatastanmadhyaantah pravilasitaroopaanapi sadaa.

Translation

When the yogi closes the house which hangs without support, the knowledge where of he has gained by the service of Paramguru, and when the chetas by repeated practice becomes dissolved in this place which is the abode of uninterrupted bliss, he then sees in the middle of, and in the space above (the triangle) sparks of fire distinctly shining.

Commentary (Avalon)

Having described the Pranava, he now speaks of its union (with chetas), i.e. Pranava yoga.

119

The yogi should close the house *(puram baddhva)*, i.e. he should, with his mind set on the act, close the inner house or, in other words, he should make yoni mudra in the manner prescribed and thus effectually close the inner house. The use of the word *pur* shows that the yoni mudra is meant. Then, when his chetas by repeated practice *(abhyasa)* or meditation on the Pranava becomes dissolved *(lina)* in this place (ajna), he sees, within and in the space above the triangle wherein the Pranava is, sparks of fire *(pavana-suhridam kanan)*. Or, to put it plainly, he sees sparks of light resembling sparks of fire appear before his mental vision above the triangle on which the Pranava rests.

It is by yoni mudra that the inner self *(antah-pur)* is restrained and detached from the outside world, the region of material sense. Manas cannot be purified and steadied unless it is completely detached from the material sphere. It is therefore that the mind (manas) should be completely detached by yoni mudra.

Yoni mudra, which detaches manas from the outside world, is thus described in *Sarada Tilaka*, "Place the left heel against the anus and the right heel on the left foot, sit erect with your body, neck and head in a straight line. Then, with your lips formed to resemble a crow's beak (kaki mudra) draw in air and fill there with your belly. Next, close tightly your ear holes with the thumbs, with your index fingers the eyes, the nostrils by your middle fingers, and your mouth by the remaining fingers. Retain the air within you *(kumbhaka)*, and with the senses controlled meditate on the mantra whereby you realize the unity *(ekatvam)* of prana and manas (i.e. recite the hamsa or ajapa mantra). This is yoga, the favourite of yogis."

That steadiness of mind is produced by restraint of breath through the help of mudra has been said by Shruti: "The mind under the influence of hamsa (the jivatma manifesting as prana) moves to and fro, over different subjects; by restraining hamsa the mind is restrained."

'Closes the house' *(puram baddhva)*: This may also mean khechari mudra. This latter also produces steadiness of mind.

As has been said, "As by this the chitta roams in the Brahman (kha) and as the sound of uttered word (tongue) also roams the ether (kha), therefore is khechari mudra honoured by all the siddhas." The chitta is *khechara* (what moves about in the sky or ether) when, disunited from manas and devoid of all worldly things, it becomes unmani. As has been said, "The yogi is united with unmani; without unmani there is no yogi." *Niralamba* means that which has no support – that from which the mind's connection with the world has been removed.

'The knowledge whereof he gained by the service of his Paramaguru' *(parama-guru-seva suviditam)*: *Parama* is excellence in the sense that he has attained excellence in yoga practice (by instructions) handed down along a series of spiritual preceptors (gurus) and not as a result of book learning. 'Serving the guru': Such knowledge is obtained from the guru by pleasing him by personal services *(seva)*; compare. "It can be attained by the instructions of the guru and not by ten million shastras."

'The abode of uninterrupted bliss' *(susukha-sadane)*: This is the place where one enjoys happiness that nothing can interrupt. This word qualifies place *(iha sthane,* i.e. ajna chakra).

'Sparks of fire distinctly shining' *(pavana-suhridam pravilasitaroopan kanan)*: These sparks of fire shine quite distinctly.

Elsewhere it is clearly stated that the Pranava is surrounded by sparks of light: "Above it is the flame-like Atma, auspicious and in shape like the Pranava; on all sides surrounded by sparks of light."

About verse 40 Avalon says that where the 'manas-ness' *(manastva)* of manas ceases to be, that is called *unmani*, the attainment of which is the secret teaching of the tantras. In quoting the respected commentator Vishwanatha on *Svacchanda Samgraha*, which speaks of unmani as above samana, he says that in unmani there is no cognition of, and no distinction is made, between kaala and kalaa; no body and no devatas and no cessation of continuity. It is the pure and sweet mouth of Rudra.

Commentary (general)

A description of khechari mudra is given in *Hatha Yoga Pradipika* (3:40–41): "One who knows khechari mudra is unafflicted by disease, unaffected by the laws of cause and effect (karma) and free from the bonds of time (death). Mind moves in Brahman (khe) because the tongue moves in space (khe). Therefore, the perfected ones have named this mudra khechari, moving in space or Brahman."

The commentary by Swami Muktibodhananda on these two verses is: "One who knows khechari mudra is one who has experienced and perfected it. The Sanskrit word *vetti*, meaning knowledge, refers to knowledge through experience, not knowledge through an intellectual concept.

"The benefits attributed to khechari mudra are those that result from experience of supra-consciousness or samadhi. Here we are told that khechari is so powerful that the practitioner can reach a state beyond karma (cause and effect), time, death and disease. These are all aspects of the influence of shakti or maya. The state of supra-consciousness is that of universal awareness, beyond duality and the finite mind. It is called kaivalya, nirvana, moksha, samadhi or Brahma. These are all synonymous terms indicating the final stage or accomplishment of raja yoga.

"Time and space are concepts of the finite mind and perception. In yoga and tantra they are said to be the tools of maya, prakriti or shakti. They are the laws of nature and finite mind is the product of nature. If you can expand the consciousness beyond the awareness of finite mind and natural phenomena, the consciousness will enter the realm of the infinite."

In his commentary, Avalon is suggesting that use of the word 'pur', meaning city, means the practitioner at this stage of experience should practise yoni mudra. Use of the word 'pur' indicates this body which has nine gates. It does not necessarily signify the practice of yoni mudra that Avalon describes in detail.

Yoni mudra is a yogic technique for closing the nine gates (eyes, ears, nostrils, mouth, urinary tract and anus) to

122

experience the mind, as it is disconnected from any external experience. However, an adept would, by concentration alone, experience this without having to practise yoni mudra.

It is clear that Avalon's comments relate to manas chakra, the place where mind is experienced without any external support (the house without support).

The bindu of the Pranava which is within the triangle is the lower bindu. Beyond this bindu lies the nada, blazing white, which is manas chakra, which is discussed separately.

So, manas chakra is the seat of chitta. It is the blazing white nada above the triangle and above the Pranava on it. Manas has two aspects, the lower and the higher. Lower manas is the product of the senses and receives the sensations via the brain and conveys them to chitta (called chetas in Avalon's text).

A possible mechanism for the creation of chitta by manas and subsequent detachment of chitta from manas, enabling manas to be 'as a house without support' or mind unsupported by any external experience could be as follows. Sense impressions are impulses that trigger brain functions, which are transformed into subtle prana vayu movements and conveyed to each chakra according to the sense in-volved. Thus odours trigger a pranic flow to mooladhara, tastes to swadhisthana, sights or form to manipura, touch to anahata and sound to vishuddhi (see 'Creation of Chitta' diagram on page 125).

In turn these pranic signals are transferred to lower manas or that aspect of mind dependent on sense stimulation. These external experiences are stored in chitta as experiences that we recall and recognize. It is here that our sense of 'I' ness identifies with the process of cognition and thus we say 'I see' or 'I smell'. Thus we can recall an experience of smell or form or colour as well as our feelings of pleasure or pain, tasteful or distasteful, desirable or undesirable. When we sleep or enter into unconsciousness, the flow of sensations to the brain ceases and thus the related petal of manas chakra is black. According to S.S. Goswami, the colours of the petals in manas chakra are yellow for smell, white for taste, red for form, ash (silver white) for touch, white for sound and black for unconsciousness.

In this verse from *Sat Chakra Nirupana* it is stated that manas is the place where chitta is absorbed, and since our attachment to the objects of chitta is always there, liberation of manas from the external experience by dissolution of chitta is only possible through the service of a Paramguru. Paramguru's role is to liberate manas from its involvement with the external guru and achieves this through understanding this process and appropriately training disciples in non-attachment and teaching the secrets of dissociating from chitta.

Manas chakra is white and has six petals. Each petal is said to represent a sense modality as well as having a representative colour. The petal representing sense of smell is yellow, sense of taste is white, sense of sight is red, sense of touch is ash, sense of sound is white and the petal representing sleep is black.

When we examine the tantric process of creation, we come to understand that creation is the evolution of the *tattwas* or elements. Since nothing comes from nothing, our consciousness plus the elements must have their essence or source in the more subtle aspects out of which they have evolved. According to tantra the five senses and the material objects evolved out of the composite mind, otherwise known as *antah karana* (manas, buddhi, chitta and ahamkara). The antah karana is the subtle source of the five *karmendriyas* (motor senses), the five *jnanendriyas* (sensory senses) and the *pancha tattwa* (five elements, being earth, water, fire, air and ether, out of which is composed the physical body and the material universe). We would therefore expect to find the subtle seeds of manifest reality in time and space in the more subtle forms of reality beyond time and space.

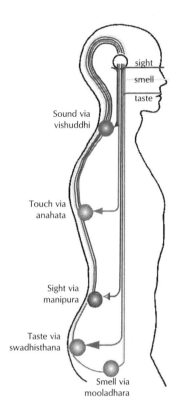

Creation of Chitta

Each sensation flows via manas in ajna to its chakra

Subtle impression of each sensation flows from its chakra to form chitta within ajna and manas

Sensation	Organ	Chakra
Smell	Nose	Mooladhara
Taste	Tongue	Swadhisthana
Sight	Eyes	Manipura
Touch	Skin	Anahata
Sound	Ears	Vishuddhi

Verse 37

Jvaladdeepaakaaram tadanu cha naveenaarkabahulaprakaasham jyotirvaa gaganadharaneemadhyamilitam. Iha sthaane saakshaad bhavati bhagavaan poornavibhavo 'vyayah saakshee vahneh shashimihirayormandala iva.

Translation

He then also sees the light (*jyoti*), which is in the form of a flaming lamp. It is lustrous like the clearly shining morning sun, and glows between the sky and the earth. It is here that the Bhagavan manifests Himself in the fullness of his might. He knows no decay, and witnesses all, and is here as he is in the region of fire, moon and sun.

Commentary (Avalon)

Yogis such as these see other visions beside the sparks of light; after seeing the fiery sparks they see the light.

'Glows between the sky and the earth' *(gagana-dharani madhya milita):* This compound adjective qualifies *jyotih* (light). *Gagana* is the sky or empty space above shankhini nadi. Shankhini nadi lies beyond ajna and all else as it is the highest nadi. yet beyond this lies the vacant space and beyond that lies unmani and nothing is beyond that. *Dharani* (earth) is the *dhara-mandala* in mooladhara. This light also extends from mooladhara to sahasrara.

He next speaks of the presence of Parama-Shiva in ajna.

'It is here' *(iha sthane):* i.e. in ajna; Parama-Shiva is here, as in sahasrara. Bhagavan is Parama-Shiva.

'In the fullness of his might' *(poorna-vibhava):* This compound word, which qualifies Bhagavan, is capable of various interpretations:

Poorna may mean complete in himself, and *vibhava*, infinite powers, such as the power of creation etc. In that case the word would mean: "One who has in him such powers, who is the absolute creator, destroyer and supporter of the universe."

Vibhava again may mean 'the diversified and limitless creation', and *poorna*, 'all-spreading'. In this sense *poorna-vibhava* means: "He from whom this all-spreading and endless (vast) creation has emanated." Compare with *Taittireya Upanishad* (3.1.1): "From whom all these originated, and in whom having originated they live, to whom they go and into whom they enter."

Vibhava again may mean omnipresence, and *poorna*, all-spreading. It would then mean: "He who in his omnipresence pervades all things."

Poorna may also mean the quality of one whose wish is not moved by the result and is not attached to any object. *Poorna-vibhava* would then mean one who is possessed of that quality.

All things except Atma pass away (the omnipresence of the ethereal region, *akasha*, etc is not ever-existent). The *Nirvana Tantra* (ch.IX) speaks of the presence of Parama-Shiva in the ajna chakra in detail: "Above this (i.e. vishuddhi) lotus is jnana lotus, which is very difficult to achieve; it is the region of the full moon, and has two petals." And, "Inside it, in the form of Hamsah, is the bija of Shambhu." And, "Thus is Hamsah in *mani-dvipa* (the isle of gems in the realm of ambrosia), and in its lap is Parama-Shiva, with *Siddha-Kali* (a form of Shakti) on his left. She is the very self of eternal bliss." By lap is meant the space within the bindus which form the visarga at the end of Hamsah.

So it has been said in describing sahasrara: "There are the two bindus which make the imperishable visarga. In the space within is Parama-Shiva." As it is in sahasrara so it is represented here (i.e. Parabindu is represented in ajna by the bindu of Omkara).

We are to understand that these two, Shiva and Shakti, are here in union *(bandhana)* in the form of Parabindu, as the letter 'Ma' *(makaratma)*, and that they are surrounded *(acchhadana)* by Maya. "She the eternal one stays here (ajna) in the form of a grain of gram and creates beings *(bhutani)*." Here the Parama-Shiva dwells in the form of a gram and, according to the *Utkaladimata*, also creates.

'As he is in the region of fire, moon and sun' *(vahneh shashimihirayor mandalamiva)*: As the presence of Bhagavan in these regions is well known, so is He here. Or perhaps the author means that as He, in the shape of a grain of gram, dwells in the regions of fire, moon and sun, in sahasrara, so does He dwell here also.

In peetha-pooja, the pooja of Paramatma and jnanatma should be performed on the mandalas of sun (Arka), moon (Indu), and fire (Agni). *Paramatma* is Parama-Shiva and *jnanatma* is jnana-shakti. The bindu should be meditated upon like the grain of gram, consisting of the inseparable couple, namely Shiva and Shakti.

Verse 38

Iha sthaane vishnoratulaparamaamodamadhure samaaropya praanam pramuditamanaah praananidhane. Param nityam devam purushamajamaadhyam trijagataam puraanam yogeendrah pravishati cha vedaantaviditam.

Translation

This is the incomparable and delightful abode of Vishnu. The excellent yogi at the time of death joyfully places his vital breath (prana) here and enters (after death) that supreme, eternal, birthless, primeval deva, the purusha, who was before the three worlds, and who is known by the Vedanta.

Commentary (Avalon)

He now speaks of the good to be gained by giving up the prana by yoga in ajna chakra.

This verse means that the excellent yogi *(yogindra)* at the time of death *(prana-nidhane)* joyfully *(pramudita-manah)* places his prana *(pranam samaropya)* in the abode of Vishnu in ajna *(iha sthane vishnoh)*, and passes away, and then enters the supreme Purusha. He describes Purusha as eternal *(nityam)*, indestructible *(vinasarahitam)*, birthless *(aja)*, primeval *(purana)*. *Deva* means he whose play is creation, existence and destruction.

'Joyfully': Glad in mind in the enjoyment of the blissful union with Atma *(atmanandena hrishta-chittah)*.

'Who was before the three worlds' *(tri-jagatam adyam)* (bhuh, bhuvah, svah): By this the implication is that He is the cause of all as He preceded all.

'Known by the Vedanta' *(vedanta-vidita)*: *Vedanta* are sacred texts dealing with the inquiry concerning the Brahman. He is known by knowledge *(jnana)* of these.

The way the prana is placed *(pranaropana-prakara)* in the place of Vishnu is described: Knowing that the time for the prana to depart is approaching, and glad that he is about to be absorbed into the Brahman, the yogi sits in yogasana and restrains his breath by kumbhaka. He then leads the jivatma in the heart to mooladhara and by contracting the anus (ashwini mudra) and following other prescribed processes, rouses kundalini. He next meditates upon the lightning-like, blissful nada, which is thread-like and whose substance is kundali *(kundalini-maya)*.

He then merges the Hamsa, which is the Paramatma, in the form of prana in the nada, and leads it along with the jiva through the different chakras according to the rules of chakra-bheda to ajna. He there dissolves all the diverse elements from the gross to the subtle, beginning with prithvi, in kundalini. Last of all, he unifies her and the jivatma with the bindu whose substance is Shiva and Shakti *(Shiva-Shakti-maya)*. Having done this, he pierces the brahmarandhra, leaves the body and becomes merged in the Brahman.

Within the ajna system

Within ajna is examined thoroughly by Goswami. He has concluded that the nada above Om is manas chakra, usually referred to in current texts on kundalini yoga as the 'raif' or the nada that is the first trace of sound consciousness.

Referring to verse 35, Avalon commented: "Above this is nada", i.e. above the Pranava is the avantara (final or second) nada, which challenges as it were the whiteness of Baladeva and the moon. By this he means to say that it is extremely white, excelling in whiteness both Baladeva and the rays of the moon."

Some read *tadaadye naado'sau* (in the place of *tadoordhve naado'sau)* and interpret it as, "Below bindu-roopi ma-kara is nada," but that is incorrect. The text says, "Above this, again, is ma-kara, shining in its form of bindu," and there is nada below it; that being so, it is useless to repeat that nada is below.

Besides, this nada is beyond the nada which forms part of the Pranava, and is part of the differentiating Para-bindu placed above the Pranava. If, however, it be urged that it is necessary to state the details in describing the special Pranava, and it is asked, "Why do you say a second nada is inappropriate?" then the reading *tadadye nado'sau* may be accepted.

129

But read thus it should be interpreted in the following manner: "This nada shown below the bindu-roopi ma-kara is bala-dhavala-sudha-dhara-samthana-hasee, and the nada first spoken of is also so described. Such repetition is free from blame on the authority of the maxim that "the great are subject to no limitations".

Whilst the maxim does hold true, in the same way that the manifest universe is an expression of the unmanifest cosmic consciousness and both manifest and unmanifest together are all pervading, total and limitless, it is also true that Goswami's comment based on his readings of the tantras does have merit.

Regarding the nada mentioned in verse 35 (the nada above Om), Goswami comments that various tantric texts state that manas mandala (manas chakra) is in the eye brow centre and (in *Yogashikhopanishad*) is in the form of a nada. These tantras are a record of the experiences of those who have walked the path of kundalini sadhana and cannot be ignored.

From the first moment consciousness dawns after unconscious sleep, that is to say from the moment we wake from unconscious sleep, we are inundated with the five external senses and sleep, and how tempting it is to fall back into sleep or to follow one of the other signals. It is only firm resolve and personal training that can help us to explore our inner depths on the higher side of manas, exploring and releasing the memories within chitta and awakening the pathways to the higher realms of consciousness.

So manas is seated in ajna and by a separation from the lowest aspect of manas (processor of sensorial information and sleep), the other aspects of manas become accessible. These other aspects are *antah karana* (manas (higher), buddhi, chitta and ahamkara).

That Acharya Swami Poornananda limited his work to a description of the six chakras does not indicate more chakras within ajna are a myth or that he did not know about them. Acharya Swami Poornananda did in fact indicate the

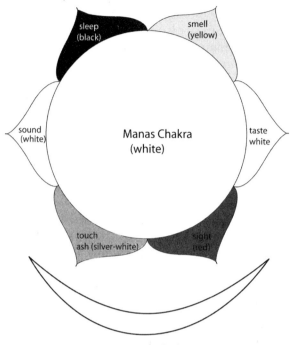

Manas Chakra

experience of manas, and his work has always been very re-
speced, studied and commented upon by many prominent
scholars.

Above manas chakra lies the sixteen-petalled indu or
shitangshu chakra. Both *indu* and *shitangshu* mean moon.
Above indu chakra lies nirvana chakra. Nirvana chakra is the
last chakra in chitrini nadi and is the highest chakra in the ajna
system. Evolution of consciousness from nirvana chakra is the
awakening of guru chakra, a sub-centre of sahasrara. Kundalini
culminates in sahasrara proper.

Summarizing, the sense nadis convey their impulses to
the five lower chakras and above them within ajna is manas.
Manas has two aspects: a lower one connected with the
senses and a higher one leading to divine or higher
experiences. Ajna is the chakra of the mind and by training,
self-control and meditation, we can transcend the attraction

of the lower senses and become absorbed in mind or manas itself without any support from external stimuli. The manas here is the whole manas or antah karana.

After indu comes nirvana chakra, and this is the last chakra within chitrini nadi, which lies within vajra and sushumna nadis, marking the end of the nadis and completing the experiences within ajna. Beyond is guru chakra, sahasrara and ultimate highest consciousness of Shiva united with Shakti, who has ascended as Ma Kundalini from mooladhara.

Nirvana chakra is the centre associated with concentration and the dissolution of the sense of 'I'. Thus the journey to the divine is beyond all duality, since there is only one and that is the experience. Swami Satyananda describes the experience in ajna as follows: "Transformation of individual consciousness is brought about by the merging of the three great forces. Individual consciousness is mainly comprised of ego, and it is on account of ego that we are aware of dualities. As long as there is duality there cannot be samadhi; as long as you remember yourself you cannot get out of yourself.

"Although there are experiences of trance in the other chakras, there is no merger of the individual ego with the cosmic ego. All throughout you are trying to assert yourself behind all the experiences you are having, but when ida and pingala unite with sushumna in ajna chakra, you lose yourself completely."

The consciousness associated with the senses in chitta persists as we continue with concentration; however, the association with the senses is replaced with a superconscious state known as 'Dhi'. The bija mantra for nirvana chakra is Gam or गं. In nirvana chakra concentration is done on lustrous Shiva.

Sat Chakra Nirupana states in verse 39: "When the actions of the yogi are, through the services of the lotus feet of the guru, in all respects good, then he will see above it (ajna) the form of the mahanada, and will ever hold in the lotus of his hand the siddhi of speech. The mahanada, which is the place of the dissolution of vayu and is half of Shiva and like

132

the plough in shape, is tranquil and grants boons and dispels fear and makes manifest pure intelligence (buddhi).

Mahanada is the place of the dissolution of all lower nadis and their source. In other words dissolution is the reverse of creation and the nadis were formed from the mahanada. It is half Shiva or *Ardhanarishwara*, the other half being Shakti, and there are countless art pieces depicting this divine state. One may question the relationship of the form of a plough to Ardhanarishwara, but we should remember the meaning of symbols is obvious in such divine states. The other interpretation favoured by Avalon is that Shiva has the mantra 'Ha' or (ह) and by removing the top part of this letter we are left with a form resembling a simple plough as drawn by a pair of oxen.

Bibliography

Goswami, S.S., *Laya Yoga*, Routledge & Kegan Paul, London, 1980

Muktibodhananda, Swami, *Hatha Yoga Pradipika*, Yoga Publications Trust, Munger, Bihar, 2002

Roney-Dougal, Serena, 'On a Possible Psycho-physiology of the Yogic Chakra System', *YOGA*, Vol 11 (3,4,5), Sivananda Math, Munger, Bihar, 2000

Saraswati, Swami Niranjanananda, *Dharana Darshan*, Yoga Publications Trust, Munger, Bihar, 2003

Saraswati, Swami Satyananda, *Asana Pranayama Mudra Bandha*, 4th (revised) edn, Yoga Publications Trust, Munger, Bihar, 2008

Saraswati, Swami Satyananda, *Dynamics of Yoga: The Foundations of Bihar Yoga*, 2nd edn, Yoga Publications Trust, Munger, Bihar, 2002

Saraswati, Swami Satyananda, *Kundalini Tantra*, Yoga Publications Trust, Munger, Bihar, 2002

Saraswati, Swami Satyananda, *Mechanics of Meditation*, 2nd edn, Bihar School of Yoga, Munger, Bihar, 1973

Saraswati, Swami Satyananda, *Meditations from the Tantras*, 2nd edn, Yoga Publications Trust, Munger, Bihar, 2000

Saraswati, Swami Satyasangananda, *Sri Vijnana Bhairava Tantra, The Ascent*, Yoga Publications Trust, Munger, Bihar, 2003

Tooley, G. A. et al, *Biological Psychology*, 53, 69–78, 71, 2000

Vivekananda, Dr Rishi, *Practical Yoga Psychology*, Yoga Publications Trust, Munger, Bihar, 2003

Woodroffe, Sir John (Arthur Avalon), *The Serpent Power*, Ganesh & Company, Madras, 2001

Glossary

Adwaita – non-dual, the concept of oneness

Agni – fire

Ajapa – involuntary unconscious repetition, especially of the mantra or sound 'soham' and 'hamso' made naturally with the ingoing and outgoing breath

Ajna – psychic command centre; the sixth chakra manifesting in the region of the midbrain

Akasha – sky matter; ether, the first of the material elements or conditions of matter; the space between the astral and physical worlds

Amrita – the nectar of immortality; another name for soma

Anahata – the fourth chakra related to the physical region of the heart

Ananda Lahari – 'Waves of Bliss'; name of a tantric text by Adi Shankaracharya

Anatma – non-self

Antah karana – internal instrument or tool of consciousness, referring to the entire mind with all its functions

Antar mouna – meditative technique of awareness of inner silence and inner 'noise'

Antar trataka – inner trataka; gazing within with the eyes closed

Anuloma viloma – mental nadi shodhana; awareness of the breath movement alternatively through the two nostrils, combined with concentration on the nosetip and trikuti

Anusthana – a fixed course of sadhana, usually practised from early morning to late night

Arani – wood used in kindling fire by friction during yajna

Ardhanarishwara – Shiva and his Shakti united in one form

Asana – seat; posture

Asat – false

Ashwini – horse; a mudra where the sphincter muscles of the anus are repeatedly contracted

Atman – the self, beyond body and mind

Aum/Om – bija mantra of ajna chakra; universal cosmic mantra

Avidya – ignorance, the root of the five kleshas

Bahiranga trataka – outer trataka, with the eyes open

Baikhari japa – audible repetition of a mantra; preliminary form of japa

Bheda – to pierce, particularly relating to the piercing of a chakra

Bija mantra – seed sound

Bindu – drop or point; dot denoting the 'n' or 'm' vowel sounds in Sanskrit; chakra manifesting in the upper posterior of the head; most important psychic centre in nada

Brahma – God as creator

Brahma sutra – chitrini-nadi

Brahmamuhurta – the auspicious time of Brahma, most suitable for meditation; the three hours preceding dawn when the atmosphere is most sattwic

Brahmarandhra – a concealed aperture in the top of the head where the kundalini leaves the body at the time of mahasamadhi

Brahmara guha – the hidden residence of Brahman; another name for ajna chakra

Bhrumadhya – eyebrow centre

Buddhi – higher intelligence, concerned with real wisdom

Chakra – wheel; centre of energy or psychic centre of the astral body

Chandra – moon; representing mental energy

Chetas – consciousness, reality

Chidakasha – inner space visualized in meditation behind the closed eyes

Chin mudra – psychic gesture of consciousness, a hand position with palm upwards on the knee and the index finger locked into the base of the thumb knees

Chitrini nadi – the main nadi of the astral body manifesting along the spinal cord; another name for sushumna

Chit – pure knowledge, beyond the division of subject and object

Chitta – empirical mind; individual consciousness; storehouse of memory; one of four aspects of antah karana; seat of consciousness, including the conscious, subconscious, unconscious and superconscious

Dama – control of the body and senses

Damaru – small hand drum

Darshan – sight, vision; philosophical system of the vedic tradition

Devata – a form of divinity; divine being having subordinate functions

Devi – female deity, goddess

Dharma – duty; code of harmonious living

Dharana – concentration or complete attention

Dhyana – spontaneous state of meditation, arising out of perfection of dharana

Drishti – seeing, viewing

Gunas – the three qualities of matter or prakriti

Guru – dispeller of the darkness of ignorance

Hakini – the goddess in ajna chakra

Hamsa mantra – mantra 'soham' or ajapa mantra

Ichchha – will; desire set by the will

Ida – psychic channel conducting pranic energy located on the left side of the psychic body; mental, lunar force; the 'tha' of hatha yoga

Idam – this; all this, as distinguished from that, or what is beyond

Indriya – an organ of sense or action

Ishta deva – the incarnate or embodied being for whom we feel an attraction and who represents the manifestation of the supreme being

Ishwara – higher reality; unmanifest existence

Itara lingam – the consolidated black shivalingam seen in ajna chakra, symbolizing the astral or subtle body

Japa – mantra repetition

Jivatma – individual self

Jnana – wisdom, higher knowledge

Jnanendriya – five subtle organs of perception: eyes, eras, skin, tongue and nose

Jyoti – inner light

Kaivalya – final liberation; highest state of consciousness beyond duality

Kaala – time

Kalaa – ray or force that manifests from the nucleus of bindu due to vibrations caused by nada

Kama – desire for material pleasures

Karma – action and result; work; law of cause and effect that shapes the destiny of each individual

Karma yoga – action performed unselfishly for the welfare of others and the fulfilment of dharma

Karmaphala – the fruit or result of action

Karmendriya – five organs of action

Kaya sthairyam – practice of absolute steadiness of the body

Khechari mudra – the attitude of moving in space; tongue lock; hatha yoga practice

Kleshas – five causes of afflictions

Koshas – sheaths or bodies

Kriya – activity associated with knowledge, leading to perfection; practices of kundalini yoga

Kula – family, lineage

Kula kundalini – primordial cosmic energy

Kumbhaka – retention of breath

Kunda – vessel, pit; starting place of kundalini

Kundalini – divine cosmic energy lying dormant in mooladhara chakra; evolutionary potential

Linga – a symbol representing Shiva, the male aspect of creation

Mahadeva – the great god; Shiva

Maha nadi – the main nadi of the astral body, otherwise called sushumna or chitrini

Maha shakti – great power

Makara – the letter 'M', the mystic syllable 'M', the third letter that concludes Aum or the pranava nada (original sound)

Mala – a bead rosary used for japa

Manas – mind; the lower aspect is connected with the senses and the higher aspect leads to higher experiences; antah karana

Manas chakra – seat of chitta

Mandala – diagram within a circumference symbolizing the deeper aspects of consciousness

Manipura – third chakra situated behind the navel in the spinal column, associated with vitality and energy

Mantra – subtle sound vibration; tantric tool which liberates energy and expands the consciousness

Mantra anusthana – an intensive day and night practice of japa

Matra – unit of time; time interval in pronouncing a sound

Maya – cause of the phenomenal world

Moha – infatuation, delusion

Moksha – liberation from the cycle of birth and death

Mooladhara – the lowest and first chakra and the seat of kundalini

Mudra – psychic attitude, often accomplished by a physical gesture, movement or posture, which affects the flow of psychic energy in the body

Mukta triveni – confluence of the three nadis, ida, pingala and sushumna, through which liberation is attained; another name for ajna chakra

Mukti – liberation from the wheel of births and deaths

Nada – subtle sound vibration heard in meditation; inner sound; prolongation of the sound in mantras such as Om; primal sound or first vibration; Omkara

Nadis – psychic channels of prana in the astral body

Nirvana – final liberation

Om/Aum – bija mantra of ajna chakra; universal cosmic mantra

Padma – lotus

Para – beyond; superior, higher

Paramatma – cosmic soul or consciousness

Parananda – celestial joy

Pingala – psychic channel conducting pranic energy located on the right side of the psychic body; solar force; the 'ha' of hatha yoga

Pooja – worship

Prakasha – brilliance, light of consciousness

Prakriti – manifest and unmanifest nature

Prana – vital energy force

Pranava – another word for the sacred syllable Aum / Om; primal sound vibration

Pranayama – yogic practices using the breath to control the flow of prana in the body

Pratyahara – sense withdrawal; the point in yoga sadhana at which the mind turns inward and progress becomes automatic

Prithvi – earth

Purusha – pure consciousness

Raga – attachment

Rajas – dynamism; one of the three gunas of prakriti

Sadhaka – one who practises sadhana; spiritual aspirant

Sadhana – spiritual discipline or practice

Sahasrara – thousand-petalled lotus or chakra manifesting at the top of the head; abode of Shiva or superconsciousness

Samadhi – culmination of meditation; state of unity with universal consciousness

Samana – one of the five vital airs, operating in the region of the navel

Samkhya – one of the six systems of Indian philosophy

Samskaras – unconscious memories

Sandhi – union

Sandhya – ritual worship conducted at dawn, noon and evening

Sankalpa shakti – the power of will

Sannyasa – dedication; complete renunciation of mundane experiences as goals in life

Sat – true; that which really exists; attribute of the ultimate reality, or Brahman

Sattwa – luminosity, harmony; one of the three gunas of prakriti

Saundarya Lahari – a tantric prayer by Adi Shankaracharya

Shakti – primal energy; power; female aspect of creation

Shama – calming or controlling the mind

Shankara – a name of the supreme; Shiva

Shankaracharya – celebrated teacher of the Adwaita Vedanta philosophy and founder of the Dashnami order of sannyasa

Shiva – 'auspicious one'; eternal transcendental consciousness; counterpart of Shakti

Shiva lingam – oval symbol of Shiva's causal form

Shodhana – purification, of six kinds

Shoonya – void

Shruti – revealed sounds of knowledge heard in a higher state of consciousness

Siddhi – accomplishment, perfection and power

Soham – 'That am I', 'so' representing cosmic consciousness and 'ham' representing individual consciousness; mantra used in ajapa japa, said to be the unconscious repetitive prayer produced by the breath

Soma – amrit; divine nectar; plant used by the ancient rishis for spiritual awakening and immortality

Sthirata – steadiness

Sukha – pleasure; happiness

Sukshma sharira – subtle body

Swadhisthana – the second chakra corresponding to the region of the pubic area, which is characterised by a drowsy state

Swara – breathing cycle; sound or tone

Tamas – darkness, inertia; one of the three gunas of prakriti

Tantras – scriptures devoted to spiritual techniques in the form of a dialogue between Shiva and Shakti, forming a set of rules for ritual, worship, discipline, meditation and the attainment of powers for all types of people

Tapas – austerity; purification

Tattwa – 'thatness'; truth; element

Trikuti – another name for ajna chakra

Unmani – centre beyond mind and thought

Upanishads – philosophical dialogues between guru and disciple in Sanskrit

Upanshu japa – whispered repetition of a mantra

Vedas – sacred knowledge; the most ancient and authentic scriptures of sanatana dharma composed before 5,000 BC, revealed to sages and seers and expressing knowledge of the whole universe

Vedanta – philosophy of realization of Brahman; Vedanta teaches the ultimate aim and scope of the vedas

Vidya – inner knowledge

Vijnana – intuitive ability of mind

Visarga – in the Devanagri script used for Sanskrit, it is half of the 'ha' sound and is represented by ':'

Vishuddhi – the fifth chakra, manifesting in the throat region

Viveka – discrimination, especially between the real and the limited

Yajna – sacrifice; offering oblations to the fire

Yantra – a symbolic design used for concentration and meditation; the visual form of a mantra

Yoga nidra – psychic sleep

Yoni – womb, source

Yoni mudra – closing the ears, eyes, nostrils and lips with the fingers, and directing the mind inwards to listen to the inner sounds. Also known as shanmukhi mudra.